GRACE

GRACE

Raphael Moss, O.P.

With an Introduction by

Ezra Sullivan, O.P.

CLUNY

Providence, Rhode Island

Cluny Media edition, 2016

For more information regarding this title
or any other Cluny Media publication,
please write to info@clunymedia.com, or to
Cluny Media, P.O. Box 1664, Providence, RI 02901

VISIT CLUNY ONLINE AT WWW.CLUNYMEDIA.COM

Grace combines two separate works by Raphel Moss, O.P.:
Conferences on the Life of Grace and *Conferences on Grace*.

Conferences on the Life of Grace originally published
in 1900 by Kegan Paul, Trench, Trübner & Co., Ltd.

Conferences on Grace originally published
in 1900 by Kegan Paul, Trench, Trübner & Co., Ltd.

Nihil obstat:
Vincent McNabb, O.P., S.T.L.
Hugh Pope, O.P., S.T.L.

Imprimatur:
John Proctor, O.P., S.T.L., *Provincial*
Herbert Cardinal Vaughn, *Archbishop of Westminster*

ISBN: 978-1944418243

Cover design by Clarke & Clarke
Cover image: Fra Angelico, *The Madonna of Humility*,
c. 1430, tempera on panel
Courtesy of National Gallery of Art, Washington, DC

Contents

Introduction

Grace, Nature, and the Unnatural

When faced with the unprecedented destruction caused by modern evils, Catholics have generally proposed two sorts of solutions. The first has been loudly advocated by politicians and would-be philosopher kings. Their declarations and charters call for a return to human values to cure the ills of our times. They proclaim that our time is the time for a new humanism, and indeed a new humanity. Theologians and churchmen, not wanting to be left behind, have often joined these voices, adding that God, or at least religion freely exercised, can play a part in the perfection of society and the progress of the human spirit. So far this solution has not produced the expected results. Evils are increasing everywhere and the new humanism has not been keeping step. The reason for this failure, Chesterton would say, is that when one takes away the supernatural, what remains is the unnatural. This leads us to the second sort of solution: when faced with the unnatural, what must be emphasized is the supernatural. Since the 1960s, official voices have often neglected this solution; it has been ridiculed in political and ecclesiastical circles. A return to earlier times can therefore expand the horizons of our thinking. Writing well before the Communist Revolution and the World Wars and so many other evils, Fr. Raphael Moss, O.P., shows us that, whatever virtues one might find in humanistic projects, the renewal of humanity above all depends on God's grace.

In saying that we ought to emphasize the supernatural, I am not suggesting that the healing balm for the human race will come from persons endowed with "superhuman" powers to combat zombies and vampires and other monsters. Nor will supernatural help arise from gnostic sources one might discover in a New Age bookstore. Writing from the eminently profound and yet utterly sensible perspective of a student of St. Thomas Aquinas, Moss insists that God is supremely supernatural—the only being that exists above created nature—and therefore all supernatural help comes from God. The Holy Trinity transforms us by grace, a gift above nature which comes to us from the humanity of Christ as mediated through His Church. The reason why grace is so effective in responding to the unnatural is that grace presupposes nature. And it does more. It heals what is most unnatural, sin and its effects, which stem from the rejection of grace by Satan and Adam and Eve. Furthermore, grace perfects and elevates the individual so that he can connaturally participate in God's divinity (see 2 Pet. 1:4). Unlike a knight's armor, strapped onto him from outside, grace is the beginning of eternal life in us, an *interior* disposition that enables a person to perform Christ-like acts beyond the powers and ends of nature alone.

A proper understanding of grace, then, can help us to begin to address the unnaturalness that we find in the world—and, indeed, in ourselves. Moss therefore denies the error of relying too much upon ourselves, a tendency manifested in the heresies of Pelagianism and various forms of naturalism, and the opposite error of relying upon God to do everything for us without our cooperation, a tendency manifested at times in charismatic circles. The first error suggests that we can be the initiators of our salvation, or that divinization is the inherent trajectory of nature; the second error suggests that nature contributes nothing to our salvation, or even that it is totally corrupt. In contrast, a theology of grace shows us that nature is not everything, but also that it is not nothing. Knowing this, Moss employs the thought of St. Thomas Aquinas to help readers "to contemplate the workings of this supernatural life, to understand the sources of its power and energy, the means to which it has recourse in time of weakness and failure and the consequences of final triumph or defeat."

Conferences on Grace

The present work, simply titled *Grace*, comprises two series of conferences that Fr. Raphael Moss (1863–1940) delivered at Oxford University. The location of the conferences is significant, for Dominicans were present in Oxford from the time of Saint Dominic in 1221 until Henry VIII dissolved all religious houses in his kingdom in 1538. In subsequent centuries, the friars remained in England in a disparate group, until the re-establishment of Catholic dioceses over three hundred years later. Thereafter, the English Dominicans began to expand, and Raphael Moss found himself to be a contemporary of both the holy friar Vincent McNabb and his eventual superior, Bede Jarrett. Soon enough, the Dominicans were back in Oxford to spread the seeds of the Gospel, setting the stage for Jarrett's re-founding of Blackfriars in 1921.

As a well-respected theologian and a popular preacher, Moss was invited to give conferences to students in Oxford. He delivered the first series, on "The Life of Grace," in 1899. These constitute part one of the present volume, covering faith, prayer, the Sacrament of Confession, Holy Communion, the Sacrifice of the Holy Mass, Purgatory, Hell, and Heaven. An attentive reader will note that the final three conferences concern what are known as the Four Last Things, showing how the conferences had something in common with a traditional parish mission. In Hilary term of the following year, 1900, Moss preached a second series of conferences, "The Working of Grace," which constitute part two of the present volume. Subjects covered here include the necessity of grace, its nature, action, and cause, its relation to the sinner, to merit, and to eternal life.

Moss's conferences will be appreciated by a variety of readers. They are theological without delving into abstruse thought; they are doctrinal without merely repeating the Penny Catechism; they are eloquent and vivid but are more than hortatory sermons. Throughout, Moss manifests his knack for finding a good example to illustrate a deep truth articulated by Aquinas. This is not meant to be a scholarly work on grace. Moss does not treat his themes historically or with textbook rigor; there is no mention of how properly to read St. Paul's letters to the Romans and Galatians in light of the Letter of St. James, nor a discussion of Augustine's controversies about grace. Cajetan, Luther, and Calvin receive only a single mention apiece, while lesser figures go unnamed. Prominent twentieth-century theologians who dominate the field, including Barth, de Lubac, and Rahner, would come later. Perhaps the closest comparison to Moss's conferences on grace can be found in the books by Matthias Scheeben, *Nature and Grace* (German ed., 1861; English ed., 1954) and *The Glories of Divine Grace* (German ed., 1862; English ed., 1885), but the differences are almost as great as the similarities. Scheeben's works are highly original and profound explorations in speculative theology, deeply rooted in the Church Fathers such as Cyril of Alexandria and Maximus the Confessor, faithful to Aquinas but going beyond the medieval thinker, conversant with many of the thinkers listed above and their historical import. Moss's conferences hew closer to Aquinas's train of thought, are more poetic, and cover more territory than Scheeben by showing in more detail how grace relates to the sacraments, the activity of prayer, and Purgatory and Hell. In the end, Moss's work provides a helpful complement to that of Scheeben, and is more accessible in some ways. To an Irish religious sister in 1901, Fr. Bertrand Wilberforce wrote,

> My dear Sister in Christ,
>
> On the subject of Grace, I would advise you to read Father Raphael Moss's *Conferences*. They are clear and solid and in no way requiring more knowledge of theology than you possess, being delivered to youths, undergraduates.

Years afterward, Moss would be at the bedside of the dying Wilberforce. When about to administer the last rites, Moss asked if he wanted to go to confession. Wilberforce, who had a habit of weekly confession, replied, "By God's grace I am not conscious of any grievous sin. But I own I was angry with a railway porter on the way up to London." In later years, Moss would experience more fully the working of God's grace in his missionary work in Grenada and while evangelizing the Zulus of South Africa.

The Triumph of Grace

It is common for Catholics to repeat the phrase uttered by St. Thérèse of Lisieux on her deathbed, that "everything is grace," but it is less common to understand what she meant. The Carmelite nun would never have thought that evil is grace, that sin is from God, or that the natural is supernatural. Such equations would have made meaningless all of her other prayers and sacrifices, not least her prayers begging the grace of conversion for the criminal Pranzini who was condemned to death. Insofar as all things stem from an undeserved gift of God, everything is grace. But not everything is a grace that leads to heaven. God offers all of us supernatural grace sufficient for our salvation, but that sort of grace can be rejected. Some have already rejected it. As Moss says, hell is the failure of grace—not that it fails us, but that we fail to cooperate with it: "The dogma of everlasting punishment is a standing rebuke to man's self-worship."

The beauty of this volume, and its greatest value, lies chiefly in how Moss describes grace and makes it appealing to us by explaining the heights to which God calls us, the depths from which He saves us, the breadth of His work in us, and the lengths to which He goes—and to which we must go—in order to unite us with Himself eternally. Moss likes to repeat that the grace of God is everlasting life, begun on earth and consummated in heaven with Christ and all the angels and saints. Through this book, readers will acquire abundant encouragement for their spiritual lives. They will receive motivation to seek God's help, and not merely self-help. In finding divine grace, they will discover that it brings the sweetest joy humans can ever experience, for it unites us in an eternal friendship with the Father, Son, and Holy Spirit.

-Ezra Sullivan, O.P.
Feast of St. Clement, 2016
Basilica San Clemente, Rome

Part One

The Life of Grace

I

Faith: The Gate of Grace

Of all the many beautiful sayings of our Blessed Lord recorded by the evangelists, it would be hard to choose one more beautiful and more significant than that recorded by St. John in the tenth chapter of his Gospel, "I am come that they may have life, and that they may have it more abundantly" (John 10:10). These words contain the summary of all His teaching, they are the revelation of the divine designs, the explanation of the Incarnation. For our Blessed Lord was not a mere reformer or philosopher, like so many who had gone before Him and were to follow Him, whose names are written large in the history of mankind. He came indeed to change the world and to reform it, and to teach the fullness of all truth, but the results towards which His reformation and His teaching tended were not bound by the limits of this world. The "life" He came to give in such abundance was a life beyond the powers of sense and understanding, seeing that its aim, its end, its means and principles, were altogether of another and higher world. Yet it was the life for which God made us, the only life that satisfies the strange mysterious longings of our human nature, and gives our complex being its full perfection. Its beginnings are in time, its foundations and its early progress can be measured by the lapse of years and the span of mortal life, but its completion belongs to eternity, and hence we justly speak of it as supernatural. We intend in these chapters to contemplate the workings of this supernatural life, to understand the sources of its power and energy, the means to which it has recourse in time of weakness and failure and the consequences of final triumph or defeat. Vital questions, surely, and most practical, and therefore worthy of our best attention, for if "the proper study of mankind is man,"[1] we have before our minds the noblest thought of that same study when we contemplate man's real life in all its varied stages and consider the greatness and the goodness of the infinite Creator in this, the most perfect work of His hands. How many there are whose lives are failures in the worst sense of the word, simply because they are so purely natural, for to live a natural life when we are made for something supernatural is to fail most pitiably! How many others too there are, whose feet have trod these higher paths, and then strayed from them—unfinished monuments, exposed to wind and rain, and falling to decay in consequence—how often have we met with such and wondered at their folly! Like the whitened bones on the desert sand, or the buoy that floats above the sunken ship, they tell us of the dangers that beset our course, and warn us to be careful, but the clearest warnings are unheeded if we cannot understand them. We must know all we can therefore, and act upon our knowledge, and so we shall succeed, and in saying this we are only pointing to the familiar Catholic doctrine of faith and good works. Let us begin with faith.

1. Alexander Pope, "Essay on Man, Epistle II," line 2.

Faith! The very word would seem to be repugnant to the apostles and disciples of that modern craze known as free-thought. It is quite true that they know very little about it, but, no doubt, they think they know enough, and in their opinion, faith is but another word for self-abasement and self-degradation, or as Pascal crudely puts it, "Pour avoir la foi, il faut s'abetir." Could anything be more untrue or more misleading? For what do we mean by "faith"? We are speaking of course of divine faith, and the definition given in our Catechism is familiar to all of us, "Faith is believing without doubting whatever God has revealed." Yet this simple definition is clear enough and deep enough to furnish a reply to all their so-called difficulties and objections. It tells us that faith implies the assent of the mind to supernatural truths on the authority of God's word. If we accept the existence of God, we must also accept the existence of truths of the supernatural order; and whether we consider these truths objectively, and in themselves, or subjectively, with reference to our minds and the criteria on which we base our assent, we are bound to admit their absolute superiority to those which are within the natural reach of our understanding. For our assent to these truths is not based on the evidence they give of themselves, or on first principles, but rather on the infinite knowledge and truth of God, who reveals them[2]; and, for this very reason, the assent which we give to them is firmer and surer in every way than any mere natural certitude, and, without a misuse of terms, cannot possibly be called blind and unreasoning. It is quite true that the object of our act of faith is something out of sight, something which is not evident to the understanding. But while we admit all this, and

2. First Vatican Council, Session III, ch, 3.

grant most willingly that a dogma of faith cannot be known by its own intrinsic proofs, yet it can put forward such a power of what we may call extrinsic evidence, as to become at once eminently credible. Hence, as Cardinal Cajetan points out, although we cannot prove to demonstration the mysteries of faith, we can most clearly demonstrate their credibility; and as it would be simple folly to deny a fact which proves its truth by its own intrinsic evidence, so also is it foolish and most wicked to refuse assent to truths which are divine, and which by reliable extrinsic evidence proclaim themselves worthy of our credence.

Now let us try to see how necessary this faith is to everyone, and the wonderful part it has to play in our supernatural life. According to St. Paul, it is its first and most essential condition. "Without faith, it is impossible to please God, for he that comes to God must believe that He exists and is a rewarder of them that diligently seek Him" (Heb. 11:6). Faith in God therefore, and in His generous love of us, is the beginning of the spiritual and supernatural life, the life of grace; it is the gate of that bright pathway of the just, "which as a shining light goes forward and increases even unto the perfect day" (Prov. 4:18).

We have defined it as a firm assent of the mind to a truth revealed by God. It is therefore a species of knowledge or vision, by which the mind apprehends certain truths of which it would be otherwise in ignorance. For, as an eloquent French writer has so beautifully pointed out, we may distinguish three separate and distinct worlds in which the great Creator manifests Himself and His exceeding glory. He made man for Himself and for the vision of Himself face to face, but, for a time at least, the full perfection of that vision is deferred, for "we see now as in a mirror and in a dark manner" (1 Cor. 13:12); and in these three worlds, and by means of them, as by three marvelous stairways, the soul of man mounts up to the throne of God. First of all, there is the world of nature. To see the great hills towering aloft, half veiled in driving mist, or the fields and woods and gardens bathed in sunshine, to stand before the ocean and gaze out upon the mighty plain of tossing waters, to look up at night to that dark blue vault above our heads, which our great poet fitly calls "the floor of heaven, thick inlaid with patines of bright gold," to think of all these worlds separated from us and from each other by distances which can be counted only in heaven, and all following their appointed paths across the wildernesses of space—surely all this lifts up the mind and heart to God, and makes the trembling soul fall prostrate in fear and adoration at the thought of His unspeakable magnificence. Now all these wonders are revealed to us by that great power of sight, which God has given to us. It is the eye of man which leads his soul abroad, and shows him all the beauty of his earthly home. Yet of what use is the eye without the mind? What pleasure could it bring us, unless the mind were there to guide the eye and help the soul to learn its easy lesson? And so there is another world of no less beauty than the world of nature, yet utterly beyond the powers of sense, an immaterial world, of thoughts and laws and principles, to which the mind alone has access; and when the mind is wanting, when the understanding and intelligence of man forget their work, he passes by this world as ignorant of it and its lessons as the poor blind man is ignorant of the gorgeous rainbow that spans the sky above his head. But great minds, on the contrary, can find such real pleasure in these higher joys revealed to them by their keen powers of thought, that for their sake they patiently endure the loss of all beside.

It is naught to them, as Milton wrote so grandly, in his years of blindness, that earth should be in darkness, when "in a purer clime the being fills with rapture, and waves of thought roll in upon the spirit." And then, once more, beyond the world of nature and the world of knowledge there is another world higher still, and far more wonderful, to which they are but as the stepping-stones across the river to the meadow lands beyond, the supernatural world of grace. It is a world which shows us God and His infinite being, His powers and His perfections, His dealings with His creatures and His revelations of Himself, not one world only, but rather many worlds of infinite beauty and attractiveness, far, far beyond all that the eye of man can see or the heart of man imagine! How, therefore, could man hope to know its wonders, unless the great Creator and efficient cause of all, who gave him eyes to see, and a mind to understand, had not once more been at his side to help him, and, by the gift of faith, completed His own handiwork and man's perfection. This then is the place of faith, this is its sphere of work most natural and most reasonable.

Of course there is no absolute necessity obliging God to speak to us and tell us all these wonders of Himself; but once we grant that God created us and made us what we are, because of His exceeding goodness, once we grant that that same love and goodness prompted Him to raise us to a supernatural state, the end of which is nothing less than intimate union with Himself, then revelation follows as a natural consequence, and is itself the proof of love. This is the reasoning of St. Thomas. "If the end of man," he argues, "be the vision of God face to face, then must man do his best to tend to God, and cling to Him by knowledge and by love, and not by any sort of love or knowledge, but only by that which we call supernatural, because the means must be proportioned to the end."[3] But "means" which in themselves are supernatural can only be bestowed by God, and hence we have revelation and the gift of grace. So, on the other hand, the act of faith by which the soul of man accepts God's revelation is man's return of love and highest pledge of loyalty. It is the worship of the understanding, the sacrifice of our best possession, the offering of the brightest jewel in our crown in tribute at God's feet. God might have acted very differently. He could have drawn aside the veil and made His revelation so complete that not a shred of mystery remained, but then our faith would cease to be a sacrifice, much less a means of merit, or rather, to speak truly, it would cease to exist. It is impossible to believe and see at the same time.[4] We believe in the existence of Jerusalem, supposing we have never been there. We know there is a city called Oxford, and there is no sacrifice on our part or merit to be found in our admission of this geographical fact. The apostle St. Thomas refused to believe in the Resurrection; he craved that lower and more natural certainty which comes from knowledge, and so drew upon himself his Master's kind rebuke: "Because thou hast seen me, Thomas, thou hast believed. Blessed are they who have not seen and have believed" (John 20:29). Still there was a blessedness of faith which the apostle could claim, for, seeing Jesus risen from the dead, he believed in His Divinity. *Hominem vidit*, says St. Gregory, *et Deum confessus est.* He saw a man before him, and confessed Him to be God. So must it be with us. Our faith is given to us to pierce the dark-

3. *Summa Theologiae* I, q. 1, a. 1; also *Summa contra Gentiles*, I, ch. 5; III, ch. 147.
4. *ST* II-II, q. 1, a. 5.

ness of the supernatural world and manifest what otherwise would be hidden from us. It is the "evidence of things that appear not" (Heb. 9:1); a mighty power which only God can give, enabling the soul to hear the voice of God above the tumult of the world, and to accept with humble submission all that He has revealed.

But though the manifestation of supernatural truth is the first and greatest work of faith, it would be a mistake to limit it to this; and it will help us greatly to appreciate its powers and worth, as well as to reject the foolish sophisms of "free-thinkers," if we reflect upon the well-nigh universal work of faith in every plane of life. Divine faith is its highest evolution, but there is a human faith as well, and what would be our life without it? The shallow-minded men, who talk so glibly of their freedom from all mental shackles, and express so loudly their conviction that all faith is but a superstition, overlook the fact that not a day can pass for any one of them without an act of faith of some sort or another. When we study history, what is it but an act of faith? And, to descend to commoner things, so also is the reading of our daily papers. A cup of coffee in the morning is an act of faith; still more a dose of medicine. And who will call us credulous because we do not summon an experienced analyst to our breakfast table or to our bed of sickness before venturing to take to one or the other? Yet even then we should have to make an act of faith in the skill and truthfulness of the analyst. So also in our social and domestic life. How strong the bond of love that binds together parents and their children, yet what is its foundation but an act of faith? An introduction at a dinner party is a triple act of faith; in fine, wherever we go, whatever we do, however we may live, an atmosphere of faith and blind dependence upon others must surround us, and we can no more escape it than we can escape the air we breathe, and nobody calls it humbling or degrading. Yet while we are obliged to put faith in each other in this universal way, there are not wanting those who try to make us shrink from faith in God, although our faith in Him and in His word, unchangeable, eternal, can never know the doubt or shadow of a cloud which human faith must ever feel! *Humanum est errare.*

Returning then to our comparison of God's three great worlds and those distinct mysterious powers which show them and reveal them to us, it is well to note how, though distinct in every way, they yet are bound together in the closest union for mutual help and ready service. The straight oar dips into the water, and at once seems broken, but reason comes to our assistance, and reveals to us those laws of light and its refraction which explain the erring judgment of the senses. So is it with our reason and our faith. The one explains the other. We have already shown the work of reason in the act of faith. It is the reason which examines and decides the value of the motives of credibility. It is the reason which unveils to us the why and wherefore of God's revelation, the work it has to do, the need we have of it and all the good it can bestow on us. And this has ever been the teaching of the Catholic Church and of those great minds whose intellectual greatness is the harvest of her blessing and her guidance. There have been some amongst her children who have sought to minimize or even to deny the work of reason in what pertains to morals or religion, but the Church rejects their wild suggestions, and, on the contrary, has ever asserted the doctrine so magnificently developed by St. Thomas in his explanation of the opening chapter of the Epistle to the Romans,[5] and confirmed by her with all the weight of her authority in the Vatican Council. There she first of all emphatically denies the possibility of opposition between faith and reason, and then explains their close relationship. "Although faith be altogether above reason, there can never be a conflict between the two, for the same God who reveals mysteries, and infuses faith, likewise gives the light of reason to the soul, and God can never contradict Himself, nor can one truth be at variance with another. If at times such opposition seem to exist, it is either because the dogmas of faith are imperfectly understood, or the assertions of mere opinions are put forward as the dictates of reason.... And not only can faith and reason never be in opposition, but they always give each other mutual assistance, for reason shows and proves the groundwork of faith, strengthening by its light the knowledge of divine things, and faith in its turn safeguards reason from many errors, and assists it in many different ways."[6] Then she goes on to brand with her anathema all those who hold the opposite extreme, and claiming for themselves the name of "rationalists" and "free-thinkers" maintain that human reason or "free-thought" is the one and only measure and criterion of all truth.[7] "Free-thought" and "free-thinkers"! Were ever words so outraged? Faith and faith alone gives us free-thought and makes us true free-thinkers, for it is faith which shows us God the one eternal and unchanging Truth, and this is perfect liberty, as defined by Christ Himself. "You shall know the truth, and the truth shall make you free" (John 8:32). For there are golden chains which honor and adorn, as there are common fetters which

5. Thomas Aquinas, *Commentary on Romans* (1:18, 21), lecture vi.

6. First Vatican Council, Session III, ch. 4.

7. First Vatican Council, Session III, ch. 4, Canon 4.

humble and degrade. To know the truth and place its yoke upon our minds is liberty, but in the minds of these would-be philosophers we see the lowest form of intellectual slavery. We should not approve of liberty which allowed a man to pick our pockets or break into our house, but we should call it license, and the ruin of all liberty; and justly so, for civil liberty supposes laws which safeguard all just rights. And has not intellectual liberty its laws also, and does not the defiance of these laws mean intellectual license? God made us free, because He made us in His own image and likeness; and when a man professes his belief in God and in God's teaching, he declares that he allows no barrier in the way of intellectual freedom, save the barrier of God's truth! "I believe in God," he says, and in those words sums up the Magna Carta of the mind. That is the free thought for which our nature craves—far different from the state of mental chaos and confusion which is the antithesis of faith—and everywhere involves a blind obedience to the changing dictates of our own strong passions, or the opinions of the latest fashionable writer.

From the mutual relations of faith and reason we pass on to a closer consideration of the virtue of faith in itself. When we quoted the definition of faith given in the Catechism, and tried to show that it implied and proved the eminent reasonableness of such an act, we were looking at it, if we may say so, from a purely objective point of view, or, in other words, with reference to the truths proposed for our belief. It will help us greatly if we likewise try to look at it subjectively, for since we showed the act of faith to be an act of knowledge, the subject in which this intellectual act takes place, or the power which gives it being, is necessarily implied, as well as the object known. So we may say at once, that to enable us to give an assent to any supernatural truth, we stand in need of what is called the light of faith, in other words a supernatural virtue bestowed upon the understanding by Almighty God. This is a defined dogma of the Church,[8] and follows from the very meaning of the definition. An absolutely supernatural truth is one which is beyond the reach of any mind, actually existing or even possible, unless its natural powers be supplemented by an additional gift which we call the light of faith. It is a light because it manifests certain truths, a light of faith, because, as we have shown above, these truths cannot be demonstrated by their own intrinsic evidence. The act of faith is therefore an act of knowledge, elicited by the understanding, strengthened by this supernatural power, and moved thereto by an act of the will.[9] It is an act of the understanding, because its object is a revealed truth, and truth is the natural object of the mind. But it is an act which is due to the influence of the will, because the object of faith is a hidden truth, and therefore is incapable of causing an assent of the mind, or that entire adhesion which is certitude. Hence the knowledge which there is in faith accompanies the assent, but is not its necessary cause, and this explains the rationale of temptations against faith. So, concludes the Angelic Doctor, the intellect concurs in the act of faith by the assent of adhesion, and the share of the will is its consent to the adhesion of the intellect. Now note what follows. This influence of the will, having for its object a supernatural good, must be in itself a supernatural act, for the nature of an act depends upon the nature of its object, and as the will left to itself cannot be the principle of a supernatural act, it follows

8. First Vatican Council, Session III, ch. 3.

9. "Credere est actus intellectus secundum quod movetur a voluntate ad assentiendum" (*ST* II-II q. 14, a. 2).

that it must owe its action to a gratuitous supernatural help, or in other words, an actual grace from God. "To believe," says St. Thomas, summing up the whole question, "is an act of the understanding, assenting to a divine truth, being moved thereto by the will under the influence of grace."[10] "With the heart we believe unto justice" (Rom. 10:10).

Evidently then we cannot guard too zealously or too carefully this most precious gift of God, which like so many of God's gifts seems so dependent on our feeble care, and that we may better realize the dangers we must shun and the efforts we must make, we may take a parable from nature. When the wintry days are over, and the warmer winds of spring begin to wake the life that sleeps within the cold dark earth, the little plant slowly pushes its head above the ground, and gradually thrives and flourishes until the flower and fruit seem close at hand. Yet even then we know that it may be a failure. Perhaps day after day the hot sun beats down upon it, until the earth around it is parched and broken, and the moisture which gives it life is all dried up, and one by one the green leaves droop and fade, and the stalk bends lower and lower, until at last the plant is withered and dead. Or, on the other hand, the sun may hardly ever shine at all, but hide himself for weeks together behind the cold grey clouds, and the sweeping rain may fall incessantly, until the rich earth is turned to mud, and the roots rot away in the water. Now the soul of man is like a plant in the garden of God's supernatural world, "a tree planted by the running waters" (Ps. 1:3), and we may liken faith to the beautiful flower that crowns it, and slowly ripens into the rich fruit of good works. But we have seen what faith implies—lowliness of mind and heart, submission of will—

10. *ST* II-II, q. 2, a. 9.

self-surrender therefore carried to its uttermost limit, and all this is very hard to flesh and blood. For there is ever whispering in the fallen heart of man the secret voice of self-love and self-worship, urging him to rise up against his Maker and tell Him to His face, *Non serviam*—"I will not obey!" (Jer. 2:20). If the soul listens and consents, the result is obvious. The soft falling rain of grace will cease, the heavens will become as brass and the earth as iron, and the heart becomes as hard as a rock, so that faith, which is the beginning of the spiritual life, seems quite impossible. We have an instance of this in the Egyptian Pharaoh, who saw the wonderful signs wrought by Moses, and "hardened his heart" (Ex. 11:10) and would not believe. Another yet more striking instance is put before us by the Scribes and Pharisees, who listened to the preaching of the Son of God Himself and saw His miracles and would not believe. They were the wise and prudent of this world from whom were hidden the things of God to be revealed to little ones, whose hearts were humble and submissive, whereas the hearts of these blind leaders were hardened and burnt up with deadly pride. For it is just this pride of heart and mind, this independent self-sufficiency that God will destroy at any cost, because it is so hateful in His sight. He demands of us the avowal of our own littleness and dependence on Him. He exacts the humble confession of our own utter inability to look on Him face to face, and it is only when the soul has done this, it is only when she has fallen with her face in the dust, and declared her nothingness apart from Him and her readiness to accept what she cannot see or understand, it is only then that God stoops to look down upon the lowliness of His servant, and pours into the mind the glorious light of faith. We humble ourselves therefore, but only that we may be exalted by God.

Then there is another obstacle to be avoided, another dangerous enemy to our faith of whom we must beware, and this obstacle, this enemy, is in many ways more evident and easy to discover, though perhaps no less difficult to overcome. Our Blessed Lord Himself has pointed it out to us when He declared that, although He Himself, the Light of God, had come into this world to give light to them that sit in darkness, yet men fled from Him, and preferred the darkness because their deeds were evil. "For," He said, "everyone that does evil hates the light and comes not to the light, that his works may not be reproved" (John 3:20). In other words, there are some hearts so corrupted, so buried in sin, that they positively shun the light of faith, and dread its brightness, because it shows them their own moral vileness in its true colors.[11] In souls such as these there is not even the wish to believe, and, as we have said, this readiness to accept the teaching of God is the essential condition of faith. Such souls may hear of those wonderful words spoken on the green hillside of Galilee: "Blessed are the clean of heart, for they shall see God" (Matt. 5:8), but there is no answering echo in their hearts. They have no wish to "see" God, because their hearts are so unclean, so soiled with the love of all that is degrading. How can the flower of faith flourish in such a muddy soil? Slowly but most surely it must wither away and die, and leave the unhappy, uncrowned soul to be cut down and cast into the fire in punishment of a loss to which it has actually become indifferent. It is of souls like these that St. Peter speaks so indignantly, comparing them to the irrational beasts, to fountains without water, to clouds tossed about

11. Oculis aegris odiosa lux, quae puris est amabilis (St. Augustine, *The Confessions*, Book VII, 16.22).

by whirlwinds, and assuring us that for them is reserved an eternal mist of darkness (2 Pet. 2:17), the darkness of willful ignorance and unbelief in this world, and, in the next, the darkness of the hopeless loss of God.

All this, then, shows us the inevitable conclusion. Faith implies self-sacrifice. It cannot come to souls that worship self, and if it has been given to such souls, it generally fades away and dies. It only flourishes in souls that are ready to pay the price it necessarily entails. Even when God does not demand the sacrifice of the body, that we lay down our lives in martyrdom, He always demands the sacrifice of the soul, the sacrifice of the understanding and the will, as we have shown. A heavy price, our human nature cries, yet even human nature can appreciate the reward, the peace of God which surpasses all understanding. In life it gives us peace that no sorrow can destroy, like the peace that dwelt in the heart of Abraham when he led his son—his only son—towards the hill of sacrifice, and answered his inquiries with that magnificent act of faith: *Deus providebit*—"God will provide a victim" (Gen. 22:8). And that same peace of mind does but increase as we near the dark valley of the shadow of death. Look at the deathbed of the apostle of free-thought, Voltaire, an agony of misery and despair, and then turn to the passing away of that great saint and doctor, whose keen intellect had soared so high on the wings of faith, St. Thomas Aquinas. "Lull of calmness and peace," says his biographer,[12] "patient as a child, gentle as charity itself," he waited for death to come. And when the Blessed Sacrament was brought to him, "I receive Thee," he exclaimed, "the price of my soul's redemption,

12. Roger William Bede Vaughan, *Life and Labours of St. Thomas of Aquinas*, vol. 11, ch. x.

for love of whom I have studied and watched and labored. Thee have I preached, Thee have I taught, against Thee never have I breathed a word, nor am I wedded to my own opinion. In entire obedience to holy Church, I now pass out of this world." And so he was taken from the twilight of faith to the glory of the everlasting vision. So was it with all the saints, so is it, and so must it ever be with all truly great souls, no matter what their work in life may be, for their faith is common to them all, and their faith is the secret of it all. So also will it be with us if we walk in their footsteps, and this same beautiful gift of faith bestowed upon us at our baptism, shows us how to succeed by placing us at the entrance of that narrow way leading to the eternal home, where we shall see our Maker face to face. The journey may seem long and tedious, and full of strange and unexpected turnings, and our souls may grow weary and our hearts fail us in the darkness, but faith will ever guide us safely and surely, and enable us to cry out bravely when our poor human nature seems tried beyond its strength, "Lord, I believe. Help Thou my unbelief."

II

Prayer: The Voice of Grace

If we admit that man was created by Almighty God, and created for no other end than to know, love, and serve his great Creator, we are also obliged to admit the duty of prayer. For it is faith, as we have seen, which enables man to know God as He wishes to be known by us; it is faith which draws aside the veil, and shows us something of His infinite perfections, and so awakens in our hearts the love which is ever waiting to be won by all that is good and beautiful and true, and as soon as faith has done this for us, the soul expresses itself in prayer. For the knowledge of God's greatness must reveal to us our own exceeding littleness, the thought of His power will remind us of our weakness and dependence on Him, the experience of His love will win from us a return of love, and the consequence of all this is prayer. It is the first-fruit of religion. For religion, according to St. Thomas,[1] aims at binding us to God in closest union. It is a virtue which inclines us to worship our Creator, and give Him honor as the first Beginning of all things, their supreme Ruler and their Lord. To Him, as to the first unfailing principle of life, we all are bound to cling, at all times and in all places we must seek Him as our one and only end, and when in weakness and in blindness we have broken from Him by the act of sin, we are straightaway bound to seek Him out again and once more pledge our faith to Him and to His service, and without prayer all this would be impossible. We may say that prayer of some sort is the first and natural duty of man—

> For what are men better than sheep or goats
> That nourish a blind life within the brain,
> If, knowing God, they lift not hands of prayer
> Both for themselves and those who call them friend?
> For so the whole round earth is every way
> Bound by gold chains about the feet of God.[2]

Yet there are not wanting those who would endeavor to evade these just conclusions. Just as a firm belief in God and in His providence implies belief in prayer, so on the other hand the profession of unbelief, or that so foolishly miscalled "free-thought," which really is, as we said in the last chapter, the lowest form of intellectual slavery, naturally involves the denial of prayer. But there are some who loudly vaunt their faith in God and in His guiding providence, yet, with a pitiable want of logic and consistency, find fault with our belief in prayer, and hence it will be useful to do our best to see and understand the place of prayer in our religious system, and how it is the natural and legitimate consequence of faith.

---

1. *ST* II-II, q. 81, a. 1.
2. Alfred Lord Tennyson, "The Passing of Arthur," from *Ides of the King*.

In the first place it is worth our while to notice how prayer is a duty put before us by our natural instincts, quite independently of all religious teaching. It would be hard to point out any power or agency more frequent and more universal in our dealings with each other than the power and agency of prayer. Society is made up of different grades and different characters. We cannot even think of it in any other way. Some of its members are young, while others are advanced in years; some are rich, others but scantily endowed with this world's wealth, while others again are altogether destitute; some are strong and shrink from nothing, others are but weak and fearful; some achieve distinction by a sort of natural right, others tread a lower and more ordinary path. Now what is the link between all these if it be not prayer? What are the words of children to their parents but words of prayer? What is the expression of filial love, or the petition for some favor, but a prayer? When a poor man stretches out his hand for alms, what is it but a prayer? When we look upon the picture of a great man's life and praise his work, our praise is prayer. Moreover, the power of prayer increases with the weakness of the suppliant; it is the feeblest whose cry is strongest. It was not the eloquence or the arguments of Arthur which aroused the pity of his cruel uncle's messenger so much as his childish helplessness.[3] We all feel this, and act accordingly, and therefore we may justly ask, if man can pray to his fellow man or hear his prayers, why should it be otherwise with God? As truly as our conscience tells us that there is a God, so also does it tell us that He hears our prayers, and no amount of foolish reasoning or shallow arguments can stifle that conviction. Even sin,

3. William Shakespeare, *King John*, Act IV, Scene 1.

that drags us down so low, can never chain us down too low for prayer, and the "limed soul, struggling to be free," can "bow the stubborn knees" and break the "strings of steel"[4] that bind the heart, and by its prayer win back the freedom it has lost. It is this inward faith in prayer which explains its universal use, so that even heathen nations have their gods and pray to them, and there never yet was found a race of men so savage or so debased as to have lost all knowledge of the use of prayer. But putting thoughts like these aside, for after all we can afford to pass them by since we are Christians, let us try to understand what our religion teaches us on this important subject. We have already stated it in brief in the opening words of this chapter, but now we may go into it more deeply.

The highest and the noblest gift bestowed upon us by our Maker is the power of understanding. In the beginning God made man, and He made him in His own image and likeness; that is to say, He gave him a spiritual nature dowered with intelligence and free will; and even when the shining light of faith is absent, that same intelligence is strong enough to pierce the clouds of ignorance and error and see something of that dazzling Sun of glory from which it draws its life and being. With faith to help it, it can see much more. By faith the soul knows God, His being and His attributes and infinite perfections, His boundless wisdom, His almighty power, His unfailing love; and knowing this and seeing this, it cries aloud in wonder and amazement: *Te Deum laudamus*—"We praise Thee, O God, we confess Thee to be the Lord." For the soul to refuse this homage would be to deny its nature and oppose the impulse of its being, for

---

4. Shakespeare, *Hamlet*, Act III, Scene 8.

God Himself has made it for no other end. Not that He has any need of it or of its praise and worship. God is God, and therefore self-sufficing. No mind that He has ever made or could make knows Him as He knows Himself, and His own self-knowledge is His own most perfect hymn of praise. But when His love broke in upon the silence of eternity, and creatures sprang from nothing at His word of power, it was and could be for no other end than His great glory. "Thus saith the Lord God, He that created the heavens and stretched them out, He that spread forth the earth and the things that spring out of it, He that gives breath unto the people upon it, and spirit to them that tread thereon… I am the Lord, that is my name, I will not give my glory to another" (Is. 42:5–8). He could not do it, almighty though He is, or rather because He is almighty, and therefore the one and only God, the first Beginning and last End of all. Man therefore lives and breathes that He may glorify his Maker by his worship and his adoration, and this worship and this adoration is the first great act of prayer.

But God has given to man another power, as we have already said, and from this second power He likewise looks for tribute. Great and wonderful as is the gift of understanding, it is but the half of that most generous dowry given to man at his creation. There is the will, the affection of the heart, as it is called, and this is taken captive in its turn by God's exceeding goodness. He is goodness itself, and we exist, with all we have and all we are, simply because God is so good. "Every best gift and every perfect gift is from above, coming down from the Father of lights," in whose love "there is no change nor shadow of turning" (James 1:17). But here again the same conclusion stares us in the face. "The Lord has made all things for Himself" (Prov. 16:4). "God's goodness," says St. Thomas, "is the final cause of all things,"[5] and he goes on to explain how, though the benefit accruing to the creature from the enjoyment of God's gifts may be called the motive of creation (*finem operis*), yet the motive of the Creator (*finem operantis*) could be none other than Himself; and the Church herself proclaims this truth in her sacred liturgy when she calls upon us to adore "the King, for whom all things exist." *Regem cui omnia vivunt, venite adoremus.* It follows therefore that God's gifts are ours, not that we may rest in them and claim them as our own, but that, by means of them, we may be lifted up to Him who gave them in a loving act of gratitude, and in this gratitude or "thanksgiving" we find the second great act of prayer.

But to praise God for His great glory and His infinite perfections and to thank Him for His countless blessings, what else is this but loyal service, the loving worship of the mind and heart in prayer? And so the Angelic Doctor tells us it is man's peculiar work, his special office in the great scheme of creation, *oratio est proprium rationalis creaturae.*[6] An old Eastern legend tells us that when God had made the world and fashioned it so fair and beautiful that even He, the great Creator, saw that it was very good, He showed it to the ministering angels gathered round His throne and bade them say if aught was wanting to its full perfection, and one of them, in bold humility obeying God's behest, declared that there was one thing lacking, and one only, and that one thing was an eternal living voice wherewith the world might glorify its Maker. This then is man's great work, a work that he alone can do; for though the holy Scriptures tell us that the

5. *ST* I, q. 44, a. 4.
6. *ST* II-II, q. 83, a. 10.

"heavens show forth the glory of God" (Ps. 18:2) that "the earth adores Him and chants His praises" (Ps. 45), though His three faithful servants standing in the fiery furnace of the Babylonian King called upon all the works of the Lord to praise and exalt Him above all forever (Dan. 3), though the ever-living Church re-echoes their hymn of praise until the end of time, and daily bids the sun and moon and stars of heaven, the earth and seas and rivers and all living things to bless and praise the Lord. Yet in this universal hymn of worship, the best and highest and most perfect voice is wanting if man be silent, for man alone can seek the inspiration of his song in his abounding knowledge; he alone can let it sound from the depth of an understanding heart; in him alone it is the outcome of free will, and nothing less than this is real praise and real glory.[7] Someone has compared the earth, as it swings on its appointed path through space, to a great thurible before the throne of God. Man's prayer is surely the sweet smelling incense in which God finds delight.

All this seems clear enough, and were man still in his unfallen state it would suffice to prove whatever we have ventured to assert; but sin has found a place upon the earth, and with sin, suffering of every kind; and therefore mingled with the homage of its praise and its thanksgiving there rises ever in God's sight the pleading cry of our poor suffering race: "Lord, save us, we perish" (Matt. 8:25). Not here or there, or once or twice in a long lifetime, but everywhere from first to last man feels the touch of sorrow; failure and disappointment dog his steps, and lest he should despair and give up struggling, hope speaks to him of prayer, and bids him ever raise his eyes to the mountains, whence help will surely come

7. *ST* I-II, q. 2, a. 3.

to him in his dark hour if he but ask for it (Ps. 121). There is no other way. God will not treat us as He treats the lower world of nature, and force His gifts upon us by a law of blind necessity; much less can feeble man presume to claim what he requires and take it by main force! God's honor is as real as man's liberty. Hence there remains a third way, the way of persuasion, which we call prayer, a power which often wins the victory when other means have failed. So Homer tells us[8] how King Priam knelt before Achilles and begged him to restore the body of Hector, and how the sight of that old man, kneeling before him and kissing the hand that had slain his dearest son, moved Achilles to forego his oath and show some pity and respect to his dead enemy. Is God less pitiful than man? St. James assures us that "the prayer of a just man avails much" (James 5:16), and the great Bossuet would have us set no limits to its power, seeing that in prayer man clothes himself in God's omnipotence.[9] Manifestly then, if prayer is a solemn duty imposed upon us by our position as creatures, it is also an undeniable need. Even if man could stifle all the nobler instincts of his nature, closing his eyes to God's perfections and shutting his heart against God's blessings, he still must feel the smart of suffering obliging him to go to God for help and comfort and relief.

Yet it is here that we part company with many who would shrink from calling themselves unbelievers, but who fail to see how prayer of this sort and God's providence can work together, so false and so distorted is their idea of God

8. *Iliad*, 24.592–93.

9. "L'homme revêtu de la toute-puissance de Dieu." Jacques Bénigne Bossuet, *Oeuvres complètes de Bossuet* (Besançon: Outhenin-Chalandre, 1836), vol. 3, p. 217.

and the workings of His providence. This prayer of petition, they say, is useless and impossible, so we must try to explain how it is neither one nor the other. And first of all we may point out that it is God who makes this law of prayer, a law most natural, most reasonable in every way, for the God we worship is the supremely intelligent Being, not a mere impersonal collection of the blind forces of nature, and therefore we believe that He ever treats His creatures in accordance with the nature He has given them. The little grain of wheat owes its being to Him, and depends on Him as absolutely as does the highest archangel. It has no knowledge of existence, and can ask for nothing as it lies buried in the cold earth, yet God, who "covers the heavens with clouds and prepares rain for the earth, who makes the grass to grow upon the mountains, and herbs for the service of men" (Ps. 147:8), remembers it, and sends the rain and the life-giving sunshine; and the answer of the buried grain of wheat, unconscious though it be, is seen in the waving field of golden corn.

So also the Psalmist tells us that "the young lions roar after their prey, and seek their meat from God" (Ps. 104:21), and that "He gives their food to the beasts of the field and to the young ravens that call upon Him" (Ps. 147:9). Not that the roaring of the wild beasts or the lowing of the cattle or the cries of the birds are a real prayer any more than the silence of the buried seed; but, according to St. Thomas, they are said to call upon God, because of those natural wants which move them to follow out the end for which they were made, and so partake of the divine Goodness, just as they are said to obey God when they follow the instinct by which God moves them to fulfill His purposes.[10]

10. *ST* II-II, q. 83, a. 10.

But man is surely on a higher level, and must be judged by other laws. He has the power of realizing all he needs and longs for, since his understanding, guided by the double light of reason and of faith, shows him his last end and all the means he must employ in order to attain it. It shows him his own weakness and the many possibilities of failure; it shows him God, almighty, merciful, full of love and pity; and then it tells him of the clear command which God has laid upon him: "Ask, and you shall receive." Obedience, therefore, to this law of prayer is a duty manifestly put before us by our faith and reason, here as elsewhere, working hand in hand, no less than by that daily experience and mutual intercourse of which we have already spoken. Nor may our opponents hope to found a serious objection on the ground that prayer between man and man is necessary in order to make known our wants, whereas they are already known to the all-seeing mind of God, as He Himself assures us: "Your Father knows that you have need of all these things" (Matt. 6:32). We do not beg for help from God and manifest our wants to Him because He knows them not, but rather to remind ourselves of our necessities and consequent dependence.[11] The rich man in the Gospel, counting up his gains, and full of confidence in their abundance, laying aside all care and preparing to eat, drink, and be merry, was but a type of what our fallen nature ever tends to do when cares and sorrows seem to pass us by. Animal instincts gain the upper hand, and the beast within us overcomes the man. To eat, drink, and be merry is right enough in season, but we were not made for that alone, and from time to time we need reminding that a day will come for us, as for that poor foolish glutton, when our

11. *ST* II-II, q. 83, a. 2, ad 1.

soul will be required of us. Our many needs and wants do this for us. They force God's claims upon us when we would forget them. "It is not," says St. Thomas, "that Almighty God is wanting in generosity, for He showers upon us many gifts that we have never thought of asking for, because He is so generous and so liberal in our regard; but there are many things for which He wishes us to ask, since He will only give them in answer to our prayers. He does this for our sakes, for by these prayers our faith in Him as the author of all good becomes more real, and our hope and trust in Him are wonderfully strengthened."[12] Then the Angelic Doctor goes on to show how prayer is eminently calculated to increase the virtue of religion in our hearts, since it implies this spirit of submission and dependence upon God for all good things.[13]

But, our opponents insist, granting all this to be as true as it is plausible, there is another difficulty in the way, which seems to prove the utter uselessness of prayer. God, they say, is of His very nature quite unchangeable, for change of any sort implies potentiality and imperfection, and God, according to the teaching of the Catholic faith, is what we call a pure act, absolutely simple and infinitely perfect, incapable therefore of any sort of change.[14] Moreover, this eternal "fixity" applies to all His attributes. His knowledge is unchangeable; the things that were are still before His mind, the things that are not yet are visible to Him. He cannot learn or be informed of anything. So also with His will. It is infinitely free, and yet eternally determined. "The counsel of the Lord," says the Psalmist, "stands forever" (Ps. 33:10);

12. *ST* II-II, q. 83, a. 2, ad 3.
13. *ST* II-II, q. 83, a. 3.
14. *ST* I, q. 9, a. 1.

and by the mouth of His prophet God Himself declares: "I am God, and there is no God beside me.... My counsel shall stand, and all my will shall be done" (Is. 46:9–10). But once we grant all this, and all who believe in God must grant it, it seems impossible to admit the utility of prayer. If God must listen to me and grant my prayer, He must in equal justice hearken to the prayers of countless millions, often contradicting one another in their petitions; and in face of such a state of things what would become of God's unchanging will and those most wonderful and equally unchanging laws by which the universe is governed? Surely, if we pray at all, our prayers should be confined to acts of worship and thanksgiving, and submission to the dread, unknown, inevitable future, already fixed and ruthlessly determined by God's will. What a religion, what a God this teaching puts before us, or rather what an ignorance of God and all religion in those who follow it! Yet these theories are not new. Six hundred years ago St. Thomas calmly weighed them, and examined them, and rejected them as worthless, in words as brief as they are clear and convincing. "The use of prayer," he says, "does not in any way interfere with the absolute freedom of the creature or the unchangeable will of the Creator. In order to see this clearly we must remind ourselves that the eternal Providence of God not only determines beforehand the various things that are to take place, but it also predetermines and prearranges their various causes and mutual relations. Amongst these different sorts of causes we must naturally include human actions. It follows therefore that when men do certain things, their actions by no means interfere with the divine pre-arrangement, but on the contrary, by these very actions they bring to pass certain effects in the way that God desires. And this is the way in which we must look at prayer.

We do not pray in order to change God's arrangement of our lives, but rather to bring to pass that arrangement which God has decreed to bring to pass by means of our prayers; or, as St. Gregory says, "By their prayers men fit themselves to receive the gifts which the Almighty from all eternity has decreed to give them."[15]

The fallacy of our opponents, therefore, consists in ignoring the great law of prayer, the law of cause and effect, while they so loudly vaunt their admiration for the laws of God in general—an intellectual position so illogical and foolish, that even Voltaire scoffs at it. Look at the world of nature. Far from being a sort of register of hard and fast laws, each restricted in action and effect to one particular sphere, it is rather a marvelous union of forces working together on what we may call the principle of give and take. Forces which at one time seem to work together, at another show themselves in opposition; sometimes they combine to overcome a third, while at another they produce a state of equilibrium. There is a law by which a solid or a liquid suddenly converted into vapor must find room for its expansion, and this it sometimes does with such terrific energy as to destroy the strongest obstacle. But the intellect of man has made that law subservient to his wants, and uses it to drive the locomotive or the steamship, as well as for the more destructive purposes of modern artillery. So also in the sphere of medicine. How many thousands have been slain by epidemics of smallpox? Now vaccination well-nigh puts an end to any danger, whatever Boards of Guardians may say. It looks as though the physical world were in revolt against the rule of man, but man possesses powers by which he may subdue it once

15. *ST* II-II, q. 83, a. 2.

again. Why may we not apply our argument to the moral world? "You cannot bring a solitary objection against prayer," says a great French philosopher, "that does not also strike at medicine or science. This sick man, you say, will either die or not, and therefore prayer is useless. But, I retort, then medicine is also useless; why trouble about doctors? Where is the difference? It is simply a question of cause and effect. The man's death or his recovery depends upon the use of certain remedies, and this condition is included in God's eternal decree."[16] Why should not God also have decreed that the man would recover in answer to fervent prayer? Nor can we call this "interference" on the part of God, or relegate it to the sphere of miracles. It is in no sense a miracle. It is the ordinary working out of the divine plan. If man's intelligence can bring one cause to bear on another, and so neutralize its effect, God knows the workings of all causes in all orders, since He is the efficient cause of all and moves them all. All the laws and all the powers and all the forces of the universe are in His hands, and hence He can employ causes which our ignorant folly would condemn as impotent, to bring about results our weakness judged to be impossible. A vast building is wrapped in darkness, and a little ignorant child stands frightened and helpless before the very keyboard of the electric light. Its father comes in answer to its call, and unhesitatingly puts out his hand, and touches one of the many ivory keys, and the whole place is flooded with light. It was only necessary to know which key to turn and to be able to reach it. There is one last objection which St. Thomas seems to hint at when he quotes the old pagan philosopher: "Noth-

16. Joseph de Maistre, *Les Soirées de St. Pétersbourg* (Lyon and Paris: J. B. Pélagaud, 1854), 1.

ing is so dearly bought as that which costs us prayers,"[17] and which modern infidelity claims as its very own. Prayer is an insult to the dignity of manhood, most lowering and degrading! "Stand up!" says Rousseau, addressing man with empty boastfulness. "You are small enough to begin with. Instead of praying, act. A beggar is always repulsive, whether he is calling upon God or man." We should hardly choose Jean Jacques Rousseau as the champion of human dignity, but it often happens that the lowest and the worst are most in evidence; and so we may consider him as representing others. Is it true then that prayer is degrading in any sense of the word? We have no excuse for those presumptuous souls who look for miracles when common sense is needed; we are not endeavoring to defend the follies of "peculiar people"; most firmly we believe that God desires us to employ all natural means, and that heaven helps those who help themselves; but there are times when the struggle seems in vain, when heart and brain are wearied with brave effort, when the waves of suffering, sorrow, and failure seem about to close above our head, and then from the tired soul there bursts the cry of faith: "Out of the depths have I cried unto Thee, O Lord!" Who can say that such a prayer dishonors or degrades? If I believe in God at all, I believe Him to be infinitely good, infinitely powerful, infinitely loving, always able, therefore, to assist, and always willing to do it, if it be good for me; and to appeal to Him in trouble, is to lift myself up and proclaim myself His child, His friend, His instrument, His fellow worker; and what honor could equal that? Through us, in us, and by us God rules the world, and brings to pass

17. Nulla res carius emitur quem quae precibu empta est (Seneca, *De Beneficiis*). Quoted in *ST* II-II, q. 83, a. 3.

His great designs, and prayer puts us in His hands. By prayer we merit, and become more pleasing in His sight and more efficient instruments for the accomplishment of His will.[18] By prayer we break the chains that hold us down to earth, and soar aloft in purer light, more fitting to our spiritual nature, where our intelligence can feed on truths that never fail, and where our heart can open out to welcome all the world. Far then from lowering him, prayer is man's patent of nobility. Raised as we are by God to the high and supernatural state of grace, with corresponding duties and rewards, it is by prayer that we fulfill the one and win the other, and so attain our real greatness and perfection. Faith shows us God, our one last End, the place of our repose, and prayer unites us to Him, so that "in Him we live, and move, and have our being" (Acts 17:28).

But if our prayer can do all this, and wields this mighty power, when it is but the feeble cry of one poor solitary heart, what must it be, and what must be its power, when it ascends from many hearts, firmly bound together in the ties of kinship; the loving praise and worship of a united home? What must it be when it is the prayer of a great nation? Above all, what must it be when all nations and all peoples unite in the grand chorus of prayer that goes up from the universal Church? It is no longer the voice of "two or three gathered together" in the name of God. It is the voice of the whole human race; or rather, it is the Bride of Christ speaking for humanity, the Spirit of God Himself inspiring her prayer and speaking with her! What then is our conclusion? Possessed as we are of the light of faith, showing us our true dignity, our work, our abundant helps, we can but blame ourselves if our

18. *ST* II-II, q. 83, a. 15.

lives are spoiled by moral failure. We are only what we are because we do not pray!

III

Confession: The Cleansing Work of Grace

When we speak about the "supernatural life of grace," we mean an earnest persevering effort to attain our last end by a loyal obedience to God's commandments, and any deliberate and willful failure on our part we unhesitatingly characterize as sinful. This is practically the definition of sin given by St. Thomas,[1] and so clear is our conviction of its truth that proof seems quite superfluous. Similarly, when the Angelic Doctor tells us that this moral failure, which we call sin, leaves a stain upon the soul, our conscience once again bears witness to the truth of his assertion. The very fact that we are reasonable beings, and that the essence of sin lies in its deviation from the law of right reason, obliges us to feel the moral humiliation which is its consequence and to acknowledge the stain it leaves upon the soul. Hence this question of sin and its consequences, and the remedies against it prepared by our Creator, must necessarily come before us when we begin seriously to consider the supernatural life. We could not pass it over even if we would. Supposing there were no such thing as sin, it would be different. Our worship of Almighty God might then indeed be limited to fervent prayers of praise and adoration, but the sad knowledge of good and evil is the fatal inheritance of our fallen race. Hence, at all times and in all places, we find men bearing witness to this fact, and in various ways, according to the best of their ability, endeavoring to undo the work of sin and blot out its dishonoring stains by rites of expiation. Our minds are therefore quite prepared to admit that in the one and only true religion, which is meant to lead our souls to God, there must be some such means provided for us. Our reason tells us that it must be so, our faith declares it is so, and bids us see and wonder at the power and wisdom and mercy of our God in the priceless sacrament of Penance.

The sacrament of Penance! It is a world of theology in itself, embracing as it does the teaching of our faith on sin and grace and the sacraments; it is perhaps the commonest of God's supernatural dealings with our souls, and yet by no means the least wonderful; it is the most beneficent of all His condescensions, and yet the very one that is the most traduced and hated. To us, on whom God has bestowed the light of faith, the need of such a sacrament seems so manifest, that we feel we could almost prove its existence to any reasonable mind by *a priori* arguments. For once we grant the possibility of sin in those who have received the grace of baptism, we are compelled to grant that another sacrament for the remission of such sins would only be what we might expect from God's great goodness, especially since it is His way to treat us in accordance with our nature and make material things the channels of His grace. It is quite true that He died to make atonement for our sins, and that

1. *ST* I, q. 63, a. 1.

His sufferings are the superabounding cause of all grace and all satisfaction.[2] But belief in His atonement does not mean that we are henceforth free to please ourselves and indulge in every sin without fear or remorse. He laid down His life for us, but, as He Himself declared (John 10:18), it was of His own free will, for no one could take it from Him, and dying for us freely, He could and did determine how the abundant fruits of all His sufferings were to be applied to the souls whom He had so generously redeemed. He instituted the sacraments. We believe that He blotted out the handwriting that was against us (Col. 2:14), and opened the closed gates of heaven to the human race; but we also believe that He laid down a clear condition, "Unless a man be born again of water and the Holy Spirit, he cannot enter the kingdom of God" (John 3:5), and hence we teach that baptism, either actually or by desire, is an essential condition of salvation. But when we grow up, and our reason and free will assert themselves, it often happens that we soon forget how much we have been favored. Freely and deliberately we turn our backs upon our Maker, and declare our independence, and even as a beautiful flower, just opening its white leaves to the bright sunshine, loses all its frail loveliness, and is sullied and destroyed when it is trampled in the dust, so also is the soul of man sullied and defiled when he consents to sin. What then can he do? He may repent, and indeed his reason tells him that repentance is essential; but is his repentance real enough to merit God's acceptance, and will He accept it? Hope says He will, but have we no visible assurance, such as God gives us in baptism? Must we be like the King of Nineveh, who hearkened to the preaching of God's prophet,

2. *ST* III, q. 48, a. 49.

and proclaimed a solemn fast, for "Who can tell," he said, "if God will turn and forgive, and turn away from His fierce anger?" (Jonah 3:9) Who can tell? There is the difficulty. So faith steps in, and tells us that there is another sacrament, "a second plank after shipwreck," a visible outward sign of the cleansing work of grace, the sacrament of Penance.

But there is another way of looking at this dogma of our faith. A sacrament is defined to be an outward sign of inward grace ordained by Jesus Christ. All its powers must come from Him, for nobody could make a sacrament, and bind the supernatural power of grace to visible things but the Author of grace Himself; and so we venture to say that any candid mind looking at this institution as an existing fact in the world, and seriously considering it, must see in it the handiwork of God, and confess it to be a sacrament, or means of grace, and a most efficient factor in the spiritual life.

In the sacrament of Penance, or "Confession" as it is commonly called amongst Catholics, we have to acknowledge two most wonderful creations utterly beyond the power of man, or any natural agency whatever. For since this marvelous institution implies the confession of one's sins to a fellow creature, it necessarily supposes the one who confesses his sins, and the one who receives the confession; the self-accused transgressor of the law and the judge who is its representative; the penitent and the confessor. Analyse these two ideas, and try to see what they imply. Who is the penitent? He is a human being, humbly avowing his sins at the feet of a fellow man. According to St. Thomas,[3] pride may be looked at as a special sin in itself, or as the fountain-head of all sin. He shows us, moreover, how it is the worst of all sins, because

3. *ST* II-II, q. 84, a. 2.

the furthest point of sin, and yet, though we may admit the reasoning of the Angelic Doctor and accept his conclusions, we cannot help feeling somehow or other that pride is the most excusable of all sins, probably because so natural to our fallen and perverted will. Miserable and poor and blind and naked as are the very best of us from a supernatural point of view, we are all, nevertheless, infected with this vice of pride. It hides itself under many forms. It often wears the robe of virtue, and the proudest man will often urge that he is only overstocked with self-respect. Yet, proud as man is by nature, stubborn and sensitive and reserved in every way, he is, by this sacrament, laid under a law which at first sight seems an outrage on human nature. For it is a law which obliges him to come and kneel at the feet of one of his fellow men—one perhaps who in the social scale may be in every way inferior and of less account, one who may be less clever, less learned, less refined—and there reveal the sins of his life. Neither age, position nor experience may avail as an excuse. All must obey. The pope himself, who claims to be the vicar of Christ on earth, is as much under the law as the youngest cleric in the Church. Kings and queens are bound equally with the poorest of their subjects. Old men bowed down by the weight of years, young men in the fierce strife of passions that make up the battle of life, children who have but begun to taste of the tree of knowledge of good and evil, all are under the same law. And they must confess all. It might not seem so hard to be obliged to confess the public crimes that outrage every law of public morals, the sins against society and its ordinances, the offenses that are committed in the light of day and under the eyes of our neighbor; but the law of confession goes further than that. All sinful acts, all moral failures and humiliations in thought, word, and deed, all are to be avowed. This is the inexorable law, and the world cries out against it as a sheer impossibility. But it is only half the wonder! Difficult as this may seem to human reason, impossible as it may appear to the world, it is surely still more difficult, still more impossible to make the confessor. For a confessor in the sacrament of Penance has not merely to listen to the self-accusation of his neighbor, and be the recipient of his confidence. His task is something far more wonderful than that; it is nothing less than superhuman! The burden laid upon him, in the exercise of this office, is beyond the strength of angels, yet in himself he is but a man as other men; like to them in body and soul and mind and heart. And what is the heart of man—the will of man? A power with high ideals, lofty aspirations, capable of heroic sacrifice, yet at the same time capable of yielding to most selfish cravings and weak enough for any fall! Manifestly, therefore, before it can undertake a work like this it must be changed, and cleansed, and strengthened until it hardly seems the same. So when Jesus Christ bestowed upon His apostles the power of forgiving sin, Holy Scripture tells us that He breathed upon them, to signify that He gave to them a new spirit, a better and more perfect heart (John 20:22). He showed them by that mysterious sign that He would have them work by His Spirit and His Heart; or, in the words of Sacred Scripture, He gave to them "wisdom and understanding exceeding much, and largeness of heart even as the sand that is on the sea-shore" (1 Kg. 4:29). The work of a confessor demands no less. For it implies a heart full of an unwearying love, a love that can bear up against the sins, the faults, the weaknesses and follies of humanity, coupled with a sense of duty that will enable him to sacrifice home and kindred and friends and pleasant occupations; or, if needful, willingly brave suffering and danger and death, often to meet with no other reward, as far as this world is concerned, than the misunderstandings, criticisms, and revilings of those whom he has tried to serve. Moreover, real and true and deep as is to be this love of souls, it may not be confined to any narrow circle. It must be ready to embrace all: the poorest of the poor as well as the rich and nobly born, the old and feeble as well as the young and light-hearted; the innocent and pure side by side with the sin-stained and the fallen. But because love is a fire which may burn and consume, it must be tempered by a purity like unto that of the angels of God, and guarded by a prudence and discretion not of this earth. Then again, these extraordinary gifts, so wonderful and so supernatural, were not to be conferred on one or two more perfect souls; but all over the world, in all nations and in all peoples, amongst the advantaged white races and the oppressed peoples of color, these representatives of Christ were to be found, so that everywhere, until the end of time, wherever sin existed, there also must be found the confessor to break asunder its chains. This is the miracle of the sacrament of Penance, and for nineteen centuries it has been before the world. Only one conclusion is possible. "This is the finger of God" (Ex. 8:19). "It is the Lord's doing, and it is wonderful in our eyes" (Ps. 117:23).

It seems hardly worth our while to insist upon a further argument; though we may pause to point it out, for it is not without its special value, and it is to be found in an appeal to history and its evidences. It has a negative as well as a positive side, and the former may be summed up in the pertinent question, "Who is the author of the practice of confession, if it be not our Lord and Savior Jesus Christ?" The Catholic Church is not unmindful of the great names in her history, the many holy pontiffs, kings and warriors, martyrs and confessors, who have deserved well of her. Their names and their achievements are ever being handed down to after ages with their fitting meed of praise; but nowhere is there mention of the one who placed within her hands this means of boundless influence. Her enemies, on the other hand, are equally silent. "Free-thought" is not the exclusive product of the nineteenth century, it has its votaries in every age, and what were they doing when this outrage on their theories was first introduced? Those others, too, whose boast it is to steer a middle course between the license of free-thought and the authority of the Church, have they no words to say, no plea of "novelties" to urge until the middle of the sixteenth century. Full five or six hundred years before the so-called Reformation, the Greeks had broken away, but the Greeks uphold confession. If we go back another six hundred years we find Nestorius, Eutyches, and others cutting themselves adrift, but never because of the dogma of confession. Surely all this silence, the silence of the centuries, speaks as eloquently as any argument, and were we now to turn to Catholic writers for the positive proofs of history, and in each succeeding age bow down before the clear, unfaltering teaching of its greatest sons; it would not be because we needed more convincing evidence, but only that we loved to hear the voice of truth triumphing over error, and proclaiming aloud to the whole world that Penance is really and truly a sacrament ordained by Jesus Christ. Passing over, therefore, the testimonies of these saints and Fathers of the Church, let us turn to the book of God's Word, and see when our Savior bestowed upon us this fresh proof of His love for our souls, and His anxiety for their salvation. Just as in the case of the Holy Eucharist, the Son of God seems to prepare the minds of His apostles for so great a gift by foretelling its bestowal, for in the eighteenth chapter of St. Matthew's Gospel, after speaking of the power of the Church, He uses these solemn words: "Amen, I say unto you, whatsoever you shall bind upon earth shall be bound also in heaven, and whatsoever you shall loose upon earth shall be loosed also in heaven" (Matt. 18:18); and then when the fitting time had come, He fulfillled His promise by conferring upon them the awful powers necessary for so great a work. The beloved disciple describes the wonderful scene: "Now when it was late that same day, the first of the week, and the doors were shut, when the disciples were gathered together for fear of the Jews, Jesus came, and stood in the midst, and said to them: 'Peace be to you.' And when He had said this, He showed them His hands and His side. Then were the disciples glad when they saw the Lord. And again He said to them: 'Peace be to you. As the Father has sent me, I also send you.' And when He had said this, He breathed on them, and said to them: 'Receive ye the Holy Spirit, whose sins you shall forgive they are forgiven them, and whose sins you shall retain they are retained'" (John 15:19–23). Every word seems to ring with a power and authority all divine. "As the Father has sent me, I also send you. Receive ye the Holy Spirit." In these words of her divine Founder, the Catholic Church has always recognized the institution of the sacrament of Penance, for they most certainly and most explicitly confer the power of forgiving and retaining sin; and hence they imply the duty of confession, for how is the divinely appointed representative of Christ to exercise His power of forgiving and retaining sins, unless the sinner himself reveal them to him.

Now let us look into this teaching of our faith more closely, and see for ourselves how perfectly it corresponds to the natural wants of man; and how, therefore, far from being a burden, it is in reality a very great help and consolation.

For if God is our last end, it follows naturally that every single law laid upon us by Him is meant to be the echo of His voice, the beckoning of His hand, now calling us onward, now warning us backwards, but ever showing us the way to Him. Hence every duty we owe to Him, every obligation under which we lie, is really meant to be a help to us. It is in absolute accordance with right reason and with our nature, and necessarily tends to perfect it by uniting it with its last end; and we assert that confession is no exception to this universal law, although we often hear it attacked by non-Catholics as unnatural and unreasonable and therefore most certainly not of God. But it is easy to prove our contention. The heart of man has been well compared to a vessel filled to overflowing, and this overflow cannot fall back upon itself, but by its very nature seeks another resting place, or, in other words, seeks and craves for sympathy. This sympathy implies confidence, and what is confession but confidence carried to its utmost limit, and made wholly supernatural by the grace of God? It also implies a fellow creature, for if we could confess to God, we should require that God should manifest Himself and His acceptance of our confidence, and, in our present state of probation, this could not be. We feel that we must lay the burden of our miseries at the feet of one like unto ourselves, and yet one who can speak to us in the name and with the authority of God Himself. Moreover, quite apart from any supernatural motive, confession is the natural instinct of a remorseful conscience. It is the soul's spontaneous and voluntary rejection of evil. But when we pass into the supernatural order, and consider it as the remedy for sin, the violation of God's law, then is its fitness even yet more clearly manifest. For in every serious sin we can discern two elements, a turning away from God, who is our last end, and a turning to the creature; in other words, the rejection of the Creator for the creature.[4] The turning away from God is the outcome of pride. Our fallen nature tends to worship self, and craves to be its own master that it may please itself and its own inclinations at whatever cost. It was this love of self which the devil aroused in our first parents when he asked: "Why has God commanded you that you should not eat of every tree of paradise?" And then in answer to the reason given: "No, you shall not die, but in whatsoever day you shall eat thereof your eyes shall be opened, and you shall be as gods, knowing good and evil." Then came the second element of sin, the act of preference. "When the woman saw that the tree was good to eat, and fair to the eyes, and delightful to behold, she took of the fruit thereof and did eat" (Gen. 3). And so God's law was broken; for when the sinner, turning away from God and preferring some created good, finds his moral freedom barred by the divine command, he spurns it with contempt, and so these two elements combine in one foolish act of revolt.

Now look at confession. In it you will find precisely the contrary elements to those which constitute the act of sin. In opposition to pride, self-indulgence, and rebellion, it imposes on us an act of true humility and self-sacrifice, and an act of childlike obedience to God's law in the submission of the will and the sorrowful avowal of our fault. How wonderful are the ways of God! Had our divine Savior not vouchsafed to bestow it upon us, no one would have dared to dream of such a remedy; but now that He has given it, we have but to look upon it to see in it His handiwork, at once a marvelous token of His power, His wisdom and His love. Moreover, it is a special privilege, for which we cannot show ourselves

4. *ST* I-II, q. 87, a. 4.

too grateful. St. Thomas tells us[5] that the word "privilege" implies a sort of private law, or favor, granted only to a few, and though all the sacraments might justly claim the title, yet in some way it seems specially to describe the sacrament of Penance. The very beautiful chapter in the Old Testament which gives us the story of Naaman the Syrian serves as a good illustration (2 Kg. 5). Naaman was the general of the Syrian army; valiant, rich and powerful, but a leper. Amongst his many slaves there happened to be a little Hebrew girl, who understood her master's trouble, and spoke about the great prophet in her own country, and told how God had blessed him with miraculous powers, so that he was able to cure all diseases, even leprosy. So Naaman set out for the land of Israel, and having found out who this prophet was, and where he dwelt, he came to him with all his grand retinue, and made his prayer. But the prophet did not trouble to see him; he merely sent his servant with a message, directing him to bathe a certain number of times in the river Jordan, and promising, if he did so, that he would be healed. Now mark the sequel. Naaman's pride was hurt. He wanted to be healed, but he also wanted to dictate the manner of his healing. He wanted more attention and more ceremony, and he was actually returning in anger to his own country, when his servants ventured to appeal to his common sense: "If the prophet had bid thee do some great thing, surely thou wouldst have done it; how much rather what he now has said to thee, 'Wash, and thou shall be clean.'" So he obeyed God's prophet, and he was healed. The lesson is most evident: If the prophet had bid thee do some great thing, surely thou wouldst have done it. Sin is a moral leprosy. Did we

5. *ST* I-II, q. 96, a. 1, ad. 1.

but realize this, no sacrifice would be too great to get rid of it, and to recover that rectitude of soul, that cleanness of heart which we have lost; and it is our wonderful privilege to be able to win it back at what is comparatively no cost at all. Moreover, the sacrifice, such as it is, not only cleanses us from the stain of sin and heals us of our disease, but over and above this, it rewards the effort we have made, by filling the soul with a new happiness, born of a superabundance of comfort and light and the perfect consciousness of forgiveness. It gives us comfort. All sorrow comes from sin, for sin is the only real sorrow, the only real misery. With our spiritual sense so unrefined it may perhaps be hard for us to see this, but reason teaches it, and faith asserts it. St. Thomas was wont to declare that he could not understand how a person living in sin could ever smile. How can there be real peace in the heart that has knowingly turned away from its last end? But by casting out sin we recover peace, for that act of self-humiliation and self-sacrifice, by restoring grace, opens the door of the soul to its true Friend, who reveals Himself to us under the gracious name of "Paraclete," or Comforter. And with consolation comes light. By the sin of our first parents, as we showed in previous chapters, our minds have been grievously darkened, and every sin that we commit deepens this intellectual darkness; so that, like poor, blind men, we stumble along, running the risk of a fall or taking the wrong turn at every moment. Our divine Master is the Light of the world, and His word is a "lamp unto our feet" and a "light upon our path" (Ps. 118:105). "He that follows me," He has declared, "walks not in darkness, but shall have the light of life" (John 8:12). There is the public light of His authoritative teaching, and the special light of grace bestowed upon each soul in proportion to its need, enabling it to see its own littleness and narrowness and poverty; and the light of this self-knowledge does not dishearten, but, on the contrary, helps us by making us more kind and patient with ourselves and with others. Lastly, there is the sense of forgiveness, the crowning joy of all. The world never forgives. Even when the poor unfortunate who has defied its laws has paid the penalty of his rashness, he is not forgiven. The stain remains, a blot upon his life and the lives of his children. Our own conscience never forgives. "I can never forgive myself," says a man, when he realizes some irreparable mistake, and he speaks the literal truth. Our conscience never speaks of sin, but it speaks to reproach and condemn; and though we may refuse to listen, and even do our best to stifle it by pretending to believe that it is "but a word that cowards use, devised at first to keep the strong in awe," yet will a day come when it repays such wrongs with interest and seems to have "a thousand several tongues, and every tongue brings in a several tale"[6] to condemn us. But God forgives, and His forgiveness is complete and perfect. It matters not how low the fall, how far the wandering. "Whose sins you shall forgive, they are forgiven"—a truly royal pardon, begetting in the repentant soul that peace which the world cannot give, since it comes from Him who alone has the right to say: "Go in peace, thy sins are forgiven thee."

We have every right therefore to point to the sacrament of Penance as a special privilege of our holy faith, and one of the chief glories of the Catholic Church. To the priest who wields this wondrous power of binding and loosing the members of Jesus Christ it is a royal unction, consecrating him a king amongst souls, at the same time filling his heart with wonder and amazement and pity and zeal, and a readi-

6. Shakespeare, *Richard III*, Act V, Scene 3.

ness to spend himself and be spent in the service of his brethren. But, in addition to this spiritual royalty, it gives him a spiritual fatherhood, for when he sees at his feet the souls for whom His Master died, laying bare before his eyes the troubles of their souls, the human spirit dies within him to give place to something more divine, so that he may justly say with St. Paul: "I live, now not I, but Christ lives in me" (Gal. 2:20). No wonder that Luther, in the hour of his fall, hesitated to uncrown himself of this bright diadem. *Confessio miro modo placet,* he wrote, *et utilis imo necessaria est, nec vellem eam non esse in Ecclesia Christi.* But his apostasy had sown the storm, and he lived to reap the whirlwind.

We have surely said enough to prove what we advanced, and to show the special place occupied by the sacrament of Penance in that supernatural life of grace to which we have been called. We may conclude with the words of the beloved disciple: "These things we write to you that you may rejoice, and your joy may be full.... If we say that we have no sin we deceive ourselves, and the truth is not in us. But if we confess our sins, He is faithful and just to forgive us our sins, and to cleanse us from all iniquity" (1 John 1:4, 8–9).

IV

Communion: The Nourishment of Grace

Our reason tells us that Almighty God, the Creator of the universe, is not only infinite in power but also infinite in goodness; and from this St. Thomas argues, in the beginning of his wonderful treatise on the Incarnation, that as it is the nature of goodness to communicate itself to others, it is only fitting that God, who is the Supreme Goodness, should communicate Himself to His creatures in a supreme and infinite way.[1] *Quod quidem maxime fiat*, says the Angelic Doctor, *per hoc quod naturam creatam sic sibi conjungit, ut una persona at ex tribus, Verbo, anima et carne, sicut dicit Augustinus.* In this wonderful mystery God became man, and all creation bent the knee in adoration before One who was truly God and Man; yet even here His infinite goodness would not find its limitations. By the Incarnation He had joined our nature in His own, so that we, who are made a little lower than the angels, are in a manner raised above them by this act of infinite condescension on His part; for, as St. Paul says, "He took not on Him the nature of the angels, but of the seed of Abraham He takes hold." Yet He desired to do more for us. Not only did He seek a union with our nature, but also with each individual member of our race, as though His love were ever urging Him to perfect and complete that union which is the end of love and for which He made us. In God's love of His creatures, therefore, is to be found the explanation of the mystery of the Incarnation; and that same infinite love is likewise the only possible explanation of the mystery of the Blessed Sacrament, of which we have now to speak. The *blessed* Sacrament! All the sacraments are holy and blessed because of their nature and their supernatural work; but here the love of God has won so glorious a triumph that human language is unable to express it, and can only repeat *Sanctissimum Sacramentum*—the most Holy Sacrament, the Blessed Sacrament! Hence it naturally holds a special and a most important place in our brief survey of the spiritual life, completing and perfecting the good work which baptism begins, so that we should stand in need of it and its abundant blessings even if we were so happy as to have never lost our baptismal innocence,[2] and it is not too much to say that all the other sacraments are but a preparation for the Holy Eucharist.[3]

The first thing that ought to strike us when we begin to consider this uttermost pledge of God's love of us, is the variety of names that have been given to it. Although, as we have just remarked, our language finally confesses its unfitness for a subject so august, and "the Blessed Sacrament," the name which expresses the least, and therefore perhaps suggests the most, is the commonest name of all. The explanation of these

1. *ST* III, q. 1, a. 1.
2. *ST* III, q. 84, a. 6.
3. *ST* III, q. 65, a. 3, and q. 75, a. 1.

various names, as given by St. Thomas, is worthy of notice. "In three different ways," says the saint, "may we look at this Holy Sacrament. With reference to the past, it calls to mind the passion of our Lord, which was a true and real sacrifice, and hence this name is given to it as well, and we speak of it as the 'Holy Sacrifice.' With reference to the present, it shows forth the unity of the Church, of which it is the bond, and therefore it is called the 'Communion.' And lastly, with reference to the future, it is a type of that divine fruition which will be given to us in our eternal home, and since it is the way thither, we call it our 'Viaticum,' or again, the 'Eucharist'—great grace—either because the grace of God is life everlasting (Rom. 6:23), or because it gives us Christ, the author of grace."[4] But all these names assume the real presence of our Savior in this sacrament, and therefore for the greater increase of our faith in this, the central dogma of our Catholic worship, we may, with all due reverence, examine it more closely.

It goes without saying that we cannot prove the real presence of Jesus Christ in the Blessed Sacrament by any arguments which have the force of demonstration. But in the first chapter we showed that in addition to the senses and understanding, we have another source of knowledge in the supernatural power of faith, and it is by faith, and faith alone that we can penetrate the veils that shroud this mystery.[5] Nevertheless, here, as in all God's works and manifestations of Himself there is a striking fitness which appeals most strongly both to faith and reason. The Old Law, as the inspired writer reminds us, was but a "shadow of good things

4. *ST* III, q. 73, a. 4.
5. *ST* III, q. 75, a. 1.

to come" (Heb. 10:1). Its various sacrifices were a type of that most perfect sacrifice, which the Incarnate Son of God would one day make, and all their power and spiritual worth was due to that great fact. But when the New Law came to put an end to types and shadows, it seems but fitting that its sacrifices should be a reality; and that the victim offered on its altars should be in very deed and truth the Lamb of God, who takes away the sins of the world. Moreover, since it is by faith that we please God and are brought near to Him, and faith is "of all things that appear not," the more the object of faith is hidden and concealed, the more perfect will be our act of faith, and the more pleasing its sacrifice in God's sight. Hence when the apostle saw his Master standing before him in all the beauty of His risen life, and fell down at His feet with that cry of adoration, "My Lord and my God," it was the hidden Godhead which his faith confessed. He saw the humanity and believed in the divinity. "More blessed are they," said our Lord with gentle reproof, "that have not seen, and yet have believed" (John 20:29). This blessedness of faith is peculiarly ours, for in the most Holy Sacrament, Manhood and Godhead are equally concealed.

Plagas, sicut Thomas, non intueor,
Deum tamen meum Te confiteor,
Fac me Tibi semper magis credere,
In Te spem habere, Te diligere.[6]

But the true explanation of the real presence is to be found in that "exceeding love wherewith Christ has loved us." We must remember that we are speaking of love that is

6. St. Thomas Aquinas, "Adoro Te Devote."

infinite, wielding power that is infinite likewise. It was this love, as we have already said, which made the Son of God become incarnate, and because a friend delights in the society of his friends, the Son of God finds His delights amongst the children of men. His visible, bodily presence will be our reward when the time of trial is over, but while it lasts, we must walk by faith rather than by sight; and His impatient love, as though unable to wait, obliges Him to give us an abiding presence none the less real because hidden under a veil.

Se nascens dedit socium,
Convescens in edulium,
Se moriens in pretium,
Se regnans dat in praemium.[7]

Love therefore is the only explanation of this marvelous condescension on the part of God, and, if the love of God be in our hearts, our faith in it becomes an easy task. To refuse to believe in it is to deny God's love of us. For love of us God became incarnate, He who is the "Brightness of God's glory," veiled His Majesty in the bonds of weakness, and appeared in the world as a helpless little child. For love of us, He would go even further, and He veiled the winning beauty of His human nature under the whiteness of a little bread! And we? "Let us love God," says St. John, "because God has first loved us" (1 John 6:19). But how can we prove our love? By believing in His love of us, and imitating it in our feeble fashion. For love of Him we strip ourselves, not of any just rights, but of the stolen, gaudy trappings of self-love, we lay down at His

7. St. Thomas Aquinas, "Verbum Supernum Prodiens."

feet the empty claims of foolish vanity, which make us odious even in the sight of men; we hide ourselves beneath the sober garments of obedience, and placing upon our minds the chains of faith, *in lumine Tuo, videbimus lumen*—in the light He gives, our blindness disappears.

Let us turn now to the sixth chapter of St. John's Gospel, in which we have recorded the promise of the Blessed Sacrament. The Evangelist tells us first of all of the wonderful miracle of the multiplication of bread in the desert, and calls our attention to its immediate consequence. "When those men had seen what a miracle Jesus had done, they said: 'This is of a truth the prophet that is to come into the world'" (John 6:14). The Jews expected a Messiah or Savior, and the sign of His presence amongst them was to be His power of working miracles like to those of their great leader Moses. On this occasion, therefore, when our Lord had fed them with miraculous bread in the desert, the remembrance of the manna must have hashed across every mind in that great multitude, and the conclusion seemed obvious: "Of a truth this is the prophet that is to come into the world." Jesus Christ accepted the comparison, for He was the Savior and Messiah promised from the beginning, but the sign which He would give was something far more divine than the mere multiplication of bread; and on the very day following this great miracle, He declared its nature in the most emphatic language to the crowd who followed Him with such enthusiasm. "Moses gave you not bread from heaven," He said, "but my Father gives you the true bread from heaven. For the bread of God is that which comes down from heaven, and gives life to the world" (John 5:32, 33). But as the Jews understood Him to refer to some earthly sort of bread, like the manna insofar as it was food for the body only, our Lord at once explained His words, and at some length, and with the greatest clearness put before them the doctrine of the Holy Eucharist.

> "Amen, amen, I say unto you, he that believes in me has everlasting life. I am the bread of life. Your fathers did eat the manna in the wilderness, and they died. This is the bread which comes down from heaven, that if any man eat of it, he may not die. I am the living bread which came down from heaven; if any man eat of this bread he shall live forever, yea, and the bread which I will give is my Flesh for the life of the world." The Jews therefore strove among themselves, saying, "How can this man give us His Flesh to eat?" Jesus therefore said unto them: "Amen, amen, I say unto you, except you eat the Flesh of the Son of man and drink His Blood, you shall not have life in you. He that eats my Flesh and drinks my Blood has everlasting life, and I will raise him up at the last day. For my Flesh is meat indeed, and my Blood is drink indeed. He that eats my Flesh and drinks my Blood abides in me, and I in him. As the living Father has sent me, and I live by the Father, so he that eats me, the same, shall live by me. This is the bread which came down from heaven. Not as your fathers did eat manna and are dead, he that eats this bread shall live forever." (John 6:47–59).

The effect of these words of our Blessed Lord upon His audience was immediate and startling. "'This is a hard saying,' they exclaimed, an impossible doctrine, 'who can hear it, who can believe it?' And many of His disciples went back, and walked no more with Him" (John 6:66). Now if our Lord had not meant the real presence as we understand it, how strange and unreasonable must His conduct and His language appear! For He had reminded them of the manna, formed by angels, miraculous in every way, and He promised to give them something greater. How could mere bread and wine compare with such a gift? It might indeed, like the manna, be the figure of something else, but it would be incomparably the weaker figure of the two. His hearers took Him at His word, and understood Him literally, and, instead of correcting them and putting an end to their difficulties, He confirmed what He had said, and allowed them to depart. Must we say that He deceived them, or that He promised what He could not perform, He who was the Almighty God of truth? Our faith in Jesus Christ bids us see in these words of His, the promise of the Blessed Sacrament, and that same faith shows us the literal fulfillment of the promise, when on the last night of His life He took the bread and wine into His hands, and changed them into His own very Body and Blood by His word of almighty power.

We naturally turn once more to the divinely inspired words of Sacred Scripture. "Now while they were at supper, Jesus took bread and blessed and broke it, and gave it to His disciples, and said: 'Take ye and eat, this is my Body.' And taking the chalice, He gave thanks, and gave to them, saying: 'Drink ye all of this, for this is my Blood of the new testament, which shall be shed for many, unto the remission of sins'" (Matt. 26:26–27). The reformer Melanchthon compares these words to the dazzling flash of the lightning. "What comment," he asks, "can the terrified mind of man venture to make on them?" But what a strange perversion of reason is implied in those who are not ashamed to argue that when the incarnate God is heard to assert so solemnly, "This is my Body, this my Blood," He really meant us to believe that it was nothing of the kind. For us, as we have said, the real presence is a matter of faith. "If anyone," says the Council of Trent, "shall dare to deny that the Body and Blood together with the soul and the divinity of our Lord Jesus Christ are truly, really, and substantially present in the most Holy Sacrament of the Eucharist, but shall assert that they are only there virtually or as in a type or figure, let him be anathema."[8] And then again: "Since Christ our Savior declared that that which He offered under the appearance of bread, was truly His Body, the Church of God has always held, and this holy synod once again affirms, that by the consecration of the bread and the wine, the whole substance of bread is changed into the substance of the Body of Christ our Lord, and the whole substance of wine into the substance of His Blood, a change which the Church justly calls transubstantiation."[9]

With this same loyal profession of faith in our hearts and on our lips we may now reverently investigate this wonderful "mystery of faith." For it is something more than a mere presence, marvelous as that may be. We said that the only possible explanation of such a miracle was to be found in the boundless love which God has for His creatures, and that same love is the key to a yet greater mystery. For the very words of Jesus Christ, both in the promise and in its fulfillment, as well as the accidents or appearances of bread and wine which form the impenetrable veil that hides the Holy of Holies, all tend to make us understand that this sacrament is meant to be the food and nourishment of our souls, and that the mystery of the real presence is but, as it were, the stepping-stone to the mystery of communion. Hence from the

8. Council of Trent, Session XIII, ch. 8, Canon 1.

9. Council of Trent, Session XIII, ch. 4.

very early ages we find the Fathers heaping words upon words in order to impress this wonderful truth upon the minds of the faithful. They speak of the "table of the Lord," "the holy table," "the divine banquet," "the bread of the Lord," "the heavenly bread," "the cup of salvation," "the cup of life," "the holy bond of union," "the holy communion," and so on. But the Angelic Doctor seems to have surpassed them all, and sums up the whole teaching of the Church in this matter in those magnificent words which we may call the anthem of the Blessed Sacrament: "O sacred banquet, in which Christ is received, the memory of His passion is renewed, the mind is filled with grace, and a pledge of future glory is given to us."[10] Let us try to fathom some of the depths here revealed to us by the greatest of the Church's Doctors.

O Sacred Banquet! The Sacraments of the Church have been instituted for no other end than to enable us to make progress in our spiritual and supernatural life. Now there is a great resemblance between this same spiritual life and the life of the body; for, after all, material things are meant to bring home to our senses the more hidden wonders of the spiritual world. Hence, just as the life of the body begins its existence by the act of generation, and then by degrees acquires strength and energy, and has to be sustained by nourishment, so also in the spiritual life. Baptism is the new birth, our spiritual regeneration, and the Sacrament of Confirmation is meant to strengthen the soul in its new life, and fit it for its work. But something else is necessary, and so in the Holy Eucharist the soul finds that spiritual nourishment for which

10. O Sacrum convivium in quo Christus sumitur, recolitur memoria passionis ejus, mens impletur gratia, et future gloriae nobis pignus datur (Office of Blessed Sacrament).

it craves.[11] All this seems evident to common sense. Life, wherever it be found, of whatever grade or perfection it may be, is always dependent upon nourishment; and if we admit the existence of the spiritual and divine life, to which our souls are raised by the gift of supernatural grace in baptism, we seem compelled to admit the necessity of spiritual food. The one is not more wonderful than the other. What strange things science tells us of the marvelously complicated process by which the body is nourished and kept alive! Chemistry steps in, and declares that, as a matter of fact, our bodies and all material things are built up by the combination of a few primary elements, but that only increases the wonder. A little grain of wheat, itself made up of certain elements, is hidden in the earth, and straightaway it begins to live, and work, and seek out other elements by which it lives its vegetable life and at the same time gathers to itself all that is necessary for ours. It becomes our food and once more surrenders all those elements it so unerringly sought out; some being taken by the blood, others by the nerves, others again by the bones, just as our nature requires. Now if God has done all this for a life so weak and so imperfect as the life of the body, what will He not do for a life which is divine.[12] Its end and object is Himself, and so He makes Himself its food. But, because as long as this world lasts, our human nature bears the penalties of sin, and has to tread a path of life surrounded by the thorns and briars of suffering, He wisely gives us this same supernatural food in a way most fitting to our state. Not in all the pomp and majesty which surround Him on His throne at the right hand of the Father, nor yet in the dazzling

11. *ST* III, q. 73, a. 1.
12. Cf. "Partakers of the Divine Nature" (1 Pet. 1:4).

brightness with which He clothed His human nature at the moment of the Resurrection; but on the contrary in meekness and lowliness, and with a helplessness which speaks even yet more powerfully to our hearts. It is as though He had searched all the riches of creation, and finding nothing worthy of His infinite love and our inexhaustible needs, nothing good enough for souls that He had created, redeemed, and sanctified, and at the same time simple enough for hearts so weak and wavering, He appealed to His own most sacred human Heart, and its answer was the Blessed Sacrament. Most truly can we call it *sacramentum caritatis*, the sacrament of love.[13] Love, as we have said, desires union, and what union could be comparable to this? There is a union indeed, like that which binds together in the one Person of Jesus Christ the divine and human natures; but such a union would fail here because of its excess, since by it man's personality would cease to be. There is a moral union, like that which links together hearts and minds in earthly friendship, and that was not enough for love which is divine. Hence His wisdom devised and His power effected a union, which was at once most human and divine, most perfect and yet most natural; for He made His living self our nourishment, and since such food is of its very nature incomparably above us, instead of being lowered to our level and transformed by us, it conquers us and makes us like unto itself. It was this truth which transported the soul of St. Augustine. "I am the food of grown men," said the voice within his soul, "grow, and thou shall feed upon me, nor shall thou change me, like the food of thy flesh, into thee, but thou shall be changed into me." "O Truth, who art eternity," was the answering cry of his heart;

13. *ST* III, q. 73, a. 3, ad 3

"O Love, who art Truth! O Eternity, who art Love."[14] Most truly, therefore, have we here a sacred banquet, at which we assist on bended knees, seeing that the food is nothing less than the Body and Blood of Christ. "O sacred banquet, in which Christ is received!" Let us now go a step further.

The words of consecration pronounced by the rightfully ordained successors of the apostles are the self-same words as those spoken by the Savior of the world at the moment of the institution of this most Holy Sacrament. But a wonderful thing has happened! As though astounded and overwhelmed by the greatness of the mystery, the Church, by the mouth of her priests,[15] breaks in upon these sacred words: "Take ye and eat, for this is my Body. Drink ye all of this, for this is the chalice of my Blood, of the New and Eternal Testament—mystery of faith—which shall be shed for you and for many unto the remission of sins." It is as though the overpowering realization of the effect of those divine words had on the instant provoked this strange outburst of adoring fear. For think of all that is implied by these words! "One moment," says a great spiritual writer, "and there is bread in the priest's hands, and wine in the chalice on the corporal. One moment, and there is the substance of bread, with its accidents inherent in it, and it would be the grossest of idolatries to offer any manner of worship to that senseless substance. Another moment, and what was bread is God! A word was whispered by a creature, and lo! he has fallen down to worship; for in his hands is his Creator, produced there by his

14. St. Augustine, VII.10.

15. "The words *mysterium fidei*, 'the mystery of faith,' found nowhere else but in the Roman Missal, was, we are told, added as a sacred tradition preserved by St. Peter." P. Gallwey, S.J., *The Watches of the Passion* (London: Art and Book Company), vol. 1, p. 435.

own whispered word. One moment, and at the bidding of a trembling, frightened man, omnipotence has run through a course of resplendent miracles, each more marvelous than a world's creation out of nothing."[16] Yet all this is summed up in those brief words of St. Thomas: "O sacred banquet, in which Christ is received!" The instant the words of consecration are pronounced the change takes place.[17] Instead of the bread and the wine, there is present on the altar the Body and Blood of Jesus, living, glorious, and triumphant. Therefore, His majestic soul is there as well, the masterpiece of divine power and love, the treasury of supernatural gifts. Nor is this all. This human nature is inseparably united to the Person of the Eternal Word, for the one cannot be without the other; and lastly, because it is a principle of faith that in all God's beautiful works outside Himself, the Blessed Trinity of Persons work together, and where there is One Person there also are the other Two, it follows that under the veil of this most Holy Sacrament, within our grasp, as it were, yet hidden from our eyes, lives and works that mystery of all mysteries, the most blessed and undivided Trinity. "Under the veil," we said. "The Eucharistic presence," as Bishop Hedley remarks, "is meant to have a double power over our beings. It has the effect of physical sense and the effect of faith."[18] Since our Blessed Lord wished to appeal to our faith by remaining invisible, it was necessary that there should be a veil to hide Him; and on the other hand, since He desired to be

16. Frederick Faber, *The Blessed Sacrament* (Baltimore: John Murphy Co., 1855), p. 160.

17. *ST* III, q. 75, a. 7.

18. John Cuthbert Hedley, O.S.B., *A Retreat: Consisting of Thirty-three Discourses with Meditation for the Use of the Clergy, Religious, and Others* (London: Burns & Oates, 1894), p. 275.

really, truly, and substantially present, this same veil would serve to indicate the place of His hiding. Something to point Him out to us, and at the same time to hide Him from us, this was what the real presence demanded; and since He also wished to make Himself the food of our souls, He chose the veils of bread and wine. In these two material things, as in everything else of a like nature, we must clearly distinguish between the substance itself, which is hidden from the senses, and its outward visible appearances. As the Council of Trent declares in the words above quoted, it is the substance which is changed by the words of consecration; the appearances or accidents are kept to form the veil which hides even while it reveals the real presence of Jesus Christ. St. Thomas teaches that these appearances remain in their entirety,[19] supported by the power of Him who has chosen so to use them, and he replies to the foolish objection of those who would argue from this that God deceives us: "The senses," says the Angelic Doctor, "are not deceived. Their legitimate work is to judge of the accidents or outward appearances which are really and truly present before them. It is for the intellect alone to judge of the substance, and in this case the understanding is preserved from making a false judgment by the light of faith."[20] Time will not allow us to linger over the many other wonderful and most interesting truths which are the consequences of the real presence, and which St. Thomas explains to us with such clearness in his great *Summa*, but we may at least quote the lines of the "Lauda Sion," in which this same great Doctor and poet-saint sums them up in his own incomparable way:

19. *ST* III, q. 75, a. 5.
20. *ST* III, q. 75, a. 5, ad 2.

Sub diversis speciebus,
Signis tantum et non rebus,
Latent res examiae.
Caro cibus, sanguis potus,
Manet tamen Christus totus,
Sub utraque specie.
A sumente non concisus,
Non confractus, non divisus,
Integer accipitur.
Sumit unus, sumunt mille,
quantum isti, tantum ille,
Nec sumptus consumitur.
Fracto demum sacramento,
Ne vacilles, sed memento,
Tantum esse sub fragmento,
Quantum toto tegitur.
Nulla rei fit scissura,
Signi tantum fit fractura,
Qua nec status, nec statura,
Signati minuitur.[21]

To attempt to express in our own language the theological terseness of these wonderful lines of St. Thomas would be to set ourselves an impossible task. It has been well said of all his hymns that they are well-nigh "supernatural, uniting the strictness of dogma with a sweetness and a melody more like echoes of heaven than mere poetry of earth."[22]

We may now return to the anthem of the Blessed Sacrament, and briefly touch upon the remaining thoughts which

21. Cf. also *ST* III, qq. 76 and 77.

22. Faber, *The Blessed Sacrament*, p. 18.

it suggests, and without which our idea of this adorable mystery would be very incomplete. When our Lord instituted this most sacred pledge of His love for us, and for the first time uttered the solemn words of consecration, He added to them a command, full of divine power and authority, and yet at the same time of the most affectionate tenderness: "Do this," He said, "in remembrance of me." Having spoken as our God and our Savior, He now pleads as a most loving friend, and, with the very words with which He authorizes His apostles to work this miracle of love, He begs us to look upon it as a memorial of Himself and all that He has done for us.[23] We must once more remind ourselves that infinite love is the key to the mystery of which we are speaking. There are some who pretend to see in it nothing but a memorial, and they base their opinion on these very words of our Lord. What a poor idea of the love of Jesus Christ! The Blessed Sacrament is indeed a memorial, but it is one in every way worthy of the Son of God. Earthly friendship may be, and surely is the brightest sunshine of our darkened lives; yet even when it shines its brightest, there looms on its horizon the cloud that may overcast it, forgetfulness and death. Hence we try to save ourselves, and fight against the threatened darkness by every means within our power, and even when we feel that separation is at hand, most certain and inevitable, we make a last attempt to overcome its consequences by every sort of touching artifice. Not content with promises and pledges, the one we love, and whom we now must lose, will link himself to some memorial, and leave that to us, to speak for him when he is gone. And speak it will:

23. *ST* III, q. 73, aa. 5 and 82, ad 1; also Council of Trent, Session XXII, ch. 9, Canon 2, and Session XIII, ch. 2.

For while the wings of fancy still are free,
And I can view this mimic show of thee,
Time has but half succeeded in his theft—
Thyself removed, thy power to soothe me left.[24]

Yet, after all, how weak the power of such memorials, how terribly inadequate their success, when measured by our longings and our hopes! So Jesus Christ, loving us all so dearly, and foreseeing the hour of separation, loved us to the very end—*in finem dilexit*—and gave us a memorial of Himself and His great love: "Do this in remembrance of me." And what was His memorial? Not the crib in which He rested as a little child, on His first coming into our cold world, not the cross, all stained though it was with the Blood so lavishly poured forth in the hours of His death-agony, but His own real Self. "For," says St. Thomas, "a memorial is something to take the place of one's own personality, and hence, the more we can attach ourselves to it, and the more of ourselves we can put into it, the more real and perfect it will be. We try to do what we can, because our love is the shadow of God's infinite love, and we fail pitiably, because we are only human. Jesus Christ wished for a memorial because His Heart was human, and succeeded because He was God. 'Take ye and eat. This is my Body. Drink ye all of this. This is my Blood. Do this in remembrance of me.'"

A few more words and we have done. "O sacred banquet in which Christ is received, the memory of His passion is renewed, the mind is filled with grace, and a pledge of future glory is given to us!" All the sacraments are the efficient instrumental causes of grace, since they exist for no other end,

24. William Cowper, *To My Mother's Picture.*

but the Holy Eucharist has a power beyond them all, and very naturally so, since it contains the Author of all grace, and by His sacramental presence He pours upon the soul that torrent of grace let loose upon the world by the mystery of the Incarnation. "He that eats me, the same shall live by me." Moreover, since this sacrament is a real memorial of His passion, its power upon the souls of men is in all respects the same as that which so effectually blotted out the handwriting that was against us, and brought redemption to our fallen world.[25] It is given to us as food and drink for no other purpose than to make us understand that it must be to our souls what food and drink are to the body, for it is meant to give us that strength and support, that new life and those new powers of which we stand in need; in other words, it is an unfailing source of grace. "The mind is filled with grace." And because the grace of God is life everlasting, in this same most Holy Sacrament, *a pledge of future glory is given to us.*

All this grace is the promise of the glory that is to come, the fruitful seed of an eternal harvest, even as our Lord Himself declared: "He that eats this bread shall live forever." The attainment of everlasting life is the chief and principal effect of this sacrament, according to the teaching of St. Thomas.[26] For whether we look at the Holy Eucharist in itself as the Body and Blood of Christ, or whether we consider it more as a means placed at our disposal by our all-merciful God, the one end for which it ever works is the completion and perfection of man's supernatural life, the glory of the kingdom of heaven. It is the Body and Blood of Him, who by His death opened to us the gates of heaven, and so be-

25. *ST* III, q. 74, a. 1; III, q. 76, a. 2, ad 1.

26. *ST* III, q. 79, a. 2.

came the "Mediator of the New Testament," "that they that are called may receive the promise of an eternal inheritance" (Heb. 9:15). With regard to our use of it, it is, as we have said, a heavenly food, and at the same time a foretaste of that union with God to which we must aspire. It is always under the "veil," and, therefore, its delights and pleasures can never fully be appreciated here. But it is the "pledge of future glory," enabling us to wait until the appointed time. It will be to us what the heaven-sent food was to the prophet, in the strength of which he traversed the weary desert land and reached the mount of God (1 Kg. 19:8). All this is most perfectly summed up by St. Thomas, in words that are often on our lips, though rarely truly fathomed by our minds and hearts; they may serve as a fitting conclusion:

O Salutaris Hostia, quae caeli pandis ostium,
Bella premunt hostilia, da robur, fer auxilium.
Uni trinoque Domino, sit sempiterna gloria,
Qui vitam sine termino, nobis donet in Patria.

V

Holy Mass: The Fountain of Grace

The concluding thought of the last chapter was one which cannot be too clearly impressed upon our minds. It was summed up in the beautiful words of St. Thomas, and it reminded us once again that Jesus Christ, true God and true Man, is the author and source of all our grace; and since, in His loving goodness, He has vouchsafed to remain on our altars under the veils of the Blessed Sacrament, it is to this same most Holy Sacrament that He would have us look for all the grace and help of which we stand so much in need. Every poor tabernacle, therefore, is the prison house of this divine Victim, whose death on the cross blotted out the handwriting that was against us, and gave us back our heavenly inheritance; and from that same lowly hiding place He sustains us in the wearisome struggle of life, and encourages us to win a place in His everlasting home. *O Salutaris Hostia!*

> O Victim of the world's salvation,
> That wide the gates of heaven hast thrown,

The foe brings war and desolation,
Give timely aid and guard Thine own.
To Thee, in triune Godhead dwelling,
Be glory everlasting given,
Be ours the joys, the bliss unfailing,
That crown our endless life in heaven.[1]

The Blessed Sacrament is therefore the means by which our Blessed Lord carries on the work He came on earth to accomplish, the sanctification and salvation of our souls; and that we might the more easily realize His most gracious design, He gave us this great pledge of His love on the last day of His mortal life. For although He was about to withdraw His visible presence from the world, it seemed as though He could not leave us altogether; and so He veiled His Godhead and humanity beneath the sacramental species, that we might know and feel the consolation of His presence. Moreover, as St. Thomas so very justly says,[2] when friends are on the eve of being parted, the near prospect of separation seems to give a new and mightier power to their mutual love, and the last words of farewell are treasured up with the most affectionate reverence; and our Lord appealed to this most natural human feeling when He gave to His apostles this token of His love in their last hour of sorrowful farewell. But there was another reason, the most important of all. He was about to lay down His life in atonement for the sins of all the ages, past, present, and to come; and since it is only "through faith in His Blood" (Rom. 3:25) that salvation is offered to all, it was fitting that in all ages men should offer to their Creator

1. St. Thomas Aquinas, "O Salutaris Hostia," trans. Fr. Aylward, O.P.
2. *ST* III, q. 73, a. 5.

some representation of this life-giving atonement. Before His coming into this world, there were the various sacrifices of the Old Law, which were in every way, as we shall see, most perfect types of His great sacrifice; and so on the eve of their fulfillment, He looked forward to the ages yet to come, and provided them with a sacrifice which should be at once the memorial and renewal of His own. In other words, the real presence of Jesus Christ on our altars is something more than a sacrament, or an outward sign of the mysterious working of divine grace; it is a sacrifice as well, and it is this truth that St. Paul asserts so briefly and yet so forcibly when he declares that we also "have an altar" (Heb. 13:10). "We have an altar," that is to say, our churches are not merely places of prayer and devotion, they are not merely the successors of the synagogues, in which we may hear the reading of the Sacred Scriptures; but they are to us what the Temple of Jerusalem was to the Jews; they are places of sacrifice, and in them there is an altar, before which stands a consecrated priest, and on which, day by day, the blood of a victim is offered up to God. In the Temple of Jerusalem, the victim offered up was a poor trembling animal; on our altars the sacrifice appears to be of bread and wine, but, says St. Paul, "The chalice of benediction, which we bless, is it not the communion of the Blood of Christ? And the bread which we break, is it not the partaking of the Body of the Lord?" (1 Cor. 10:16) This is the great truth we have now to consider.

The doctors of the Church, and spiritual writers at various times, have suggested different derivations for the word "religion," each conveying a more or less correct idea of its meaning, but St. Thomas reminds us[3] that, whichever we

3. *ST* II-II, q. 81, a. 1.

may prefer, the virtue of religion necessarily implies the subordination of man to God. We manifest this subordination by the various acts of worship and honor, which we offer to God as the first beginning and last end of all things. Some of these acts are altogether interior, such as the raising up of the mind and heart to God in prayer, while others demand an exterior manifestation. It is not simply for God's sake that His creatures show Him honor and due reverence. Every such act implies a real blessing, the enjoyment of which is altogether our own. God is infinitely perfect in Himself, and therefore self-sufficing in every way, and creatures cannot add to His essential happiness. But by giving to the Creator that honor, praise, and worship which is His due, the creature places itself and its whole being in subjection to Him, and in this submission ever finds its own true happiness and perfection.

Now we have it on the authority of the apostle (Rom. 1:20), that it is by the visible, sensible things of this material creation, that the unseen things of God are brought home to the soul of man, for the work of his understanding depends on them to a very great extent,[4] and hence, man necessarily employs various outward and visible signs to stir up in his soul those interior acts which form the essence of religion, the first and most important of which we have already touched upon, when we treated of prayer. It is not that God has any need of them, for He can read the heart; the necessity is altogether on the side of man, and is the outcome of that nature, which leads him to manifest his thoughts by outward signs since, as we have pointed out, it is by means of outward signs and objects that he receives his knowledge. Hence

4. *ST* II-II, q. 81, a. 7.

St. Thomas concludes[5] that the duty of offering sacrifice to God is laid upon us by the law of nature, or the dictates of our own reason, since it is that same power of understanding which prompts us to make use of exterior things, and offer them to God as a token of submission and obedience and an acknowledgment of His universal dominion. For when man realizes the power of the Almighty Creator, and is filled with the sense of his own littleness and absolute dependence, the desire to express these feelings of reverence is a natural consequence, and impels him to have recourse to sacrifice. It is the highest act of worship of which the soul of a man is capable, and one which can be given to God alone; for it implies the total oblation of oneself, body and soul, to that infinite Being whom we thereby acknowledge to be our Creator and Master; it confesses Him to be the only Lord of life and death, the supreme Ruler of all things.

The very earliest records of our race show us man engaged in this most solemn act of worship, for we read in Sacred Scripture how Cain offered to God the fruits of the earth, and Abel the firstlings of the flock (Gen. 4:3–4). The first act of those who were saved from the Deluge was to offer sacrifices (Gen. 8:20) to the Lord, and the history of the patriarchs is full of similar pictures. Then came the law. It was promulgated amidst all the pomp and majesty of Sinai, in order to impress its importance upon a stiff-necked people, and, clear and distinct as is every part of it, the divine legislation with regard to sacrifice seems to stand out above all the rest in minuteness of detail. There were to be sacrifices for sin, sacrifices of thanksgiving, sacrifices of supplication, and they were not merely types and shadows and empty figures

5. *ST* II-II, q. 85, a. 1.

and ceremonies. They were ordained by the infinite wisdom of God to fulfill a double purpose.[6] Sacrifice is, as we have said, a most solemn act of worship, and these multitudinous sacrifices of the Old Law were intended, first of all, to keep alive in the hearts of the chosen people the worship of the one true God. They were a public and official recognition of the great truth, that the whole earth and the fullness thereof belonged to God, and existed but for His glory, since it was He who had given life and being to all things. "Thine are the riches," said David (1 Chr. 29:12–14), when he had gathered together all that was necessary for the building of the temple—Thine are the riches, and Thine is the glory, Thou hast dominion over all... all things are Thine, and we have but given Thee what we received of Thy hand." But what follows from this? In all these acts of sacrifice, men were but offering God's gifts back to Him, and they were His lesser gifts, the lesser tokens of His goodness, never therefore really worthy of His acceptance. A more perfect gift was to come. "God so loved the world as to give His only-begotten Son; that whoso believes in Him may not perish, but may have everlasting life" (John 3:16). Hence the best and most perfect of all sacrifices was that which was accomplished when the only-begotten Son of God offered Himself to His Father "as an odor of sweetness" (Eph. 5:2), and therefore the second purpose of the stately ceremonial of the Old Law was to shadow forth and prefigure this supreme and most complete sacrifice, in which it found its own fulfillment. And how clear was the shadowing forth! How complete the fulfillment! We read of the solemn feasts of expiation, when a poor innocent animal was brought before the high-priest, that he might lay his

6. *ST* I-II, q. 102, aa. 2 and 3.

hands upon its head, and humbly confess all the iniquities of the people, and then how it was driven forth into the wilderness to die (Lev. 16:21), the innocent victim of others' sins, and we are vividly reminded of one who took upon Himself the sins of the whole world, and atoned for them by His death, suffering "without the gate" (Heb. 13:12). Or again there was the sacrifice of the paschal lamb, so marvelously eloquent and significant. It was to be a lamb without spot or blemish, offered up by the whole people (Ex. 12); its innocent blood was to be sprinkled on the doors to ward off the vengeance of the destroying angel, and its flesh was to be eaten with unleavened bread. Who could consider this most touching rite in the afterlight of the Gospel, and not see in it with St. Thomas the most perfect type of that divine Savior, the "Lamb of God," who died for us on the cross and abides with us in the most Holy Sacrament?[7]

The sacrifice of Jesus Christ is therefore at once the explanation and consummation of all other sacrifices. He came into this world to save and redeem a fallen race, and He accomplished this by the sacrifice of Himself on the cross of Calvary. It was a mighty work, and one which He alone could do, for being both God and man, He was able to make an infinite atonement for an infinite offense, and merit for man an infinite reward. This is the necessary consequence of the Incarnation. Because He was God, every act that He performed was the act of a divine Person, and was therefore infinitely meritorious; and because He was man He was able to die for us. The motive of the Incarnation, therefore, was our redemption,[8] and at that most solemn moment when

7. *ST* III, q. 73, a. 6.
8. *ST* III, q. 1, a. 3.

"the word was made flesh and dwelt amongst us," He entered upon His office as the "one great Mediator" (1 Tim. 2:5), at once the great High Priest of the world and its Victim. "How great is Thy love for us, O tender Father," says St. Augustine,[9] "seeing that Thou hast not spared Thine only Son, but hast delivered Him up for us poor sinners... for us to Thee, both Victor and Victim, and therefore Victor because the Victim; for us to Thee, Priest and Sacrifice, and therefore Priest because the Sacrifice; making us of servants sons, by being born of Thee and serving us." We do not think enough about this glorious office of our Savior, and our faith needs something of the proud loyalty of St. Paul when he speaks of "our great High Priest Jesus, the Son of God" (Heb. 4:14). For what is a priest but a mediator between God and man, inasmuch as by his office he is obliged to be their teacher, their mouthpiece, and, in a sense, their victim. "For the lips of the priest shall keep knowledge, and they shall seek the law at his mouth" (Mal. 2:7), and he, in return, must speak to God for them, and "offer gifts and sacrifices for sins" (Heb. 5:1); and all this is pre-eminently the work of Jesus Christ.[10] But He was more than our priest. He was, as St. Augustine so beautifully puts it in the passage we have just quoted, *Sacerdos et Sacrificium, et ideo Sacerdos quia Sacrificium.* Try to realize what our Blessed Lord has done for us by His Incarnation. He was "delivered up for our sins" (Rom. 4:25), and so obtained their forgiveness; He obtains for us the grace we need, being "made for all that obey Him, the cause of eternal salvation" (Heb. 5:9), and lastly, it is only through His Blood that we can win eternal glory. But it is precisely because of our great

9. St. Augustine, *The Confessions,* Book X.

10. *ST* III, q. 22, a. 1.

need of these three favors that we have recourse to sacrifice, and that we see God in the Old Law ordaining sin offerings and peace offerings and holocausts, and therefore, concludes the Angelic Doctor,[11] our Lord and Savior was not only our great High Priest, but likewise our Victim and Sacrifice in every sense of the word. And He is our Priest and Victim forever. It is true that He can no longer suffer and die as He suffered and died on Calvary, for "death shall no more have dominion over Him" (Rom. 6:9). But besides the act of sacrifice in itself, we have to consider in the work of a priest the consummation of the sacrifice, which consists in the attainment of its fruits by those for whom it is offered, and in this sense our Lord's priesthood is eternal.[12] "Because He continues forever," says St. Paul, "He has an everlasting priesthood, whereby He is also able to save forever them that come to God by Him, always living to make intercession for us" (Heb. 7:24–25). What a wonderful thought is this, and what happiness it ought to bring to us who have the grace of faith! The death of Jesus Christ on Calvary was the central point of all creation. Around it revolved the eternal designs of God, as well as the faith and hope and love of all the hearts of men; and the ages that had gone before, as well as those that still lay hidden in the unknown future, were blessed and sanctified and consecrated in that most solemn moment when God heard the loud cry of His incarnate Son, and saw Him, Priest and Victim, die upon the altar of the cross, crimsoned with His Blood. For "He was wounded for our iniquities and bruised for our sins.... By His bruises we are healed... and the Lord has laid on Him the iniquity of us all" (Is. 53:5–6).

11. *ST* III, q. 22, a. 2.
12. *ST* III, q. 22, a. 5.

By the sacrifice of this divine Victim, the amplest atonement was made to God, and abundant grace was purchased for the cleansing of all sinful souls[13]; and, therefore, all the sacrifices that had been the types of this divine sacrifice were now fulfillled, and all necessity for future sacrifice was entirely abolished. But see the goodness of our loving God! When justice and mercy were satisfied, love yet demanded more, and "because of the exceeding love wherewith He loved us," He determined that His great sacrifice should endure until the end of time, not as a mere commemoration or as an empty ceremony, but in all its august and dread reality. Listen to the authoritative words of the Council of Trent: "Because of the imperfection of the Levitical priesthood… it was fitting, in accordance with the designs of the Father of mercies, that another Priest should arise who should be able to sanctify and make perfect all the elect, our Lord Jesus Christ Himself. And although He, our Lord and our God, would win our eternal redemption by the oblation of Himself to His Father in death on the altar of the cross, yet by death His priesthood was by no means to come to an end. Hence, at the Last Supper, on the night of His betrayal, He arranged to leave to His beloved spouse the Church, a visible sacrifice, such as our human nature requires, which should represent the sacrifice of suffering accomplished once for all on the cross, and be, at the same time, a perpetual memorial of Himself, and a means of applying His saving graces to our daily offenses. Declaring Himself, therefore, a priest forever according to the order of Melchizedek, He offered up His own Body and Blood to God the Father, under the appearances of bread and wine, and then gave it under the same symbols, as food

13. *ST* III, q. 22, a. 3.

to His apostles, whom He then and there constituted priests of the New Testament. Moreover, by the words, *Hoc facite in meam commemorationem*, He commanded them and their successors in the priesthood to offer it up in like manner, as the Catholic Church has always believed and taught. This is that clean oblation which God Himself, by the mouth of the prophet Malachi, foretold should be offered up in every place, and which can in nowise be polluted by any wickedness on the part of those who offer it. This, in fine, is the sacrifice which was prefigured by all preceding sacrifices, since it contains all the good things signified by them, and is at once their completion and perfection."[14]

In these words we have summed up, clearly, distinctly, and authoritatively, the teaching of the Catholic Church with regard to that special sacrifice of the New Testament which we call the Mass. We believe it to be the self-same sacrifice as that of Calvary, perpetuated and continued, the self-same Victim, the self-same priest, only the altar and manner of the sacrifice being changed. There is the self-same Victim; for, as the holy Council says, it is the Body and Blood of the Incarnate God, under the appearances of bread and wine, so that, although the manner of the sacrifice is changed and there is no pain, no suffering, no agony of death, no violent shedding of blood, there are nevertheless all the constituents of a true sacrifice. A sacrifice consists in the oblation of any sensible thing, which undergoes some change by being given to God and consecrated to Him, by a duly appointed minister, and the essence of the Eucharistic sacrifice lies in that mysterious change by which Jesus Christ becomes present under the sacramental veils, and offers Himself to God, His

14. Council of Trent, Session XXII, ch. 1.

heavenly Father. It is the equivalent of His death on the cross, for He becomes present on the altar as a helpless Victim, in a state which is a sort of death, and this change is sufficient for a true sacrifice. When His Mother Mary and the weeping apostles adored His lifeless Body swathed in the wrappings of the grave, He was not more helpless or more passive than when He lies on the corporal, hidden under the white veils of the sacred host. Moreover, just as His precious Blood was drained from His most holy Body on the altar of the cross, so on our altars the Body and Blood are mystically separated by that twofold consecration which is necessary to complete the sacrifice. But if the victim is the same, so also is the priest. When our Lord Himself offered this mystical sacrifice for the first time, the very words which He used called attention to the act of sacrifice: "This is my Body which is given for you; this is the Chalice, the New Testament in my Blood which is shed for you;" and then by a further exercise of His almighty power He bestowed upon His apostles a share in the character and attributes of His priesthood, and commanded them to offer the same sacrifice in remembrance of Him. They shared His power, therefore, in the sense of being its administrators and His instruments; and so at the solemn moment of the most holy Eucharistic sacrifice the individual priest who stands at the altar seems to disappear, and for the moment He clothes himself with the awful personality of the Son of God. "This is my Body," he says; "This is the chalice of my Blood." The words are the words of Jesus Christ, the act is the act of Jesus Christ, the power which effects the miracle is the power of Jesus Christ, the Incarnate God. What a privilege then is ours to possess in our midst such a manifestation of God's power and wisdom and love, such an inexhaustible fountain of richest graces. By means of the Holy Mass we can offer to God a perfect worship, and pay our debts to Him, to the very last farthing, infinite though they may be. We owe Him a debt of praise and adoration. Think of the ages that passed over the world before the Incarnation, the long centuries during which the earth had never once been able to give to its Creator an act of worship worthy of Him. For the law was laid upon it from the beginning, "Praise the Lord according to the multitude of His greatness" (Ps. 150:2), and His greatness is infinite in every way. The angels had veiled their faces in adoration; patriarchs and prophets and holy kings had wept and prayed and multiplied their sacrifices, and God stooped to accept them, simply because their very insufficiency had drawn from the bosom of the Godhead that cry of the eternal Word, *Ecce venio* (Ps. 39:8)—Behold I come—a promise to be fulfillled on Calvary, and then to go on re-echoing until the end of time on every Catholic altar.

We remember our manifold sins and their appalling consequences, and we realize that we owe to God a debt of satisfaction which far exceeds ten thousand talents, and which we can never hope to pay if abandoned to ourselves. But He who so patiently bowed His thorn-crowned head in death on the cross, by the unspeakable dignity of the Godhead which was one with Him, by the extent and intensity of the sufferings through which He passed, no less than by the exceeding love with which He welcomed them and endured them, offered to God an atonement infinitely surpassing the debts of a thousand sinful worlds. And that same sacrifice of propitiation is daily placed at our disposal in the holy Mass, for there we are once again face to face with "Jesus, the Mediator of the New Testament, and the sprinkling of blood which speaks better than that of Abel" (Heb. 12:24). He pleads for us, and intercedes for us, and obtains for us not only the forgiveness of our sins, but likewise the many graces and helps of which we stand so much in need.

What then must be our thanksgiving? When we think of all God's gifts to us—gifts in the order of nature,—our life, our health, our strength, our friends, our homes, our many joys, past, present, and to come—gifts in the order of grace,—our faith and its priceless consequences—we are forced to ask with the royal prophet, *Quid retribuam*—"What shall I give back to the Lord for all he has given to me," and then hearken to the inspired answer, *Calicem salutaris accipiam*—"I will take the chalice of salvation, and I will call upon the name of the Lord." At best, we can but lift to heaven sin-stained heads and sin-stained hearts, we can but give to God the remnants of our spoiled and wasted lives; but when the priest in the Mass offers up in our name the chalice of salvation, he offers to God the praise and thanksgiving of Him, by Whom God has given to us all these good things, and through Whom and in Whom likewise, He receives all honor and glory. "Through Christ our Lord, by whom, O Lord, thou dost ever create, sanctify, quicken, bless, and give us all these good things. Through Him and with Him and in Him, is to thee, God the Father Almighty in the unity of the Holy Spirit, all honor and glory."[15] For when the awful mystery is accomplished, and Jesus is "transfigured" before us, though so very differently from that transfiguration on the mountain top in the days of His mortal life, yet faith is quick to see His glory, veiled beneath the whiteness of His sacramental garments, and hears from out the cloud the voice of the eternal Father, "This is my beloved Son, in whom I am well pleased" (Matt. 17:5).

15. Canon of the Mass.

What then should be our devotion to the holy Mass? What should be the place in our thoughts and in our lives given to Jesus in the Blessed Sacrament? It was at the foot of the altar that St. Thomas found the secret of all holiness and purity and intellectual greatness, for holiness of soul and cleanness of heart and true knowledge go hand in hand, and God is the giver of these as of all other good gifts. But He only gives them to those who seek Him and prefer Him before all His gifts. "Well hast thou written of me, Thomas," said the voice of Jesus to the Angelic Doctor, "well hast thou written of me! What shall be thy reward?" "Lord," replied the saint, "naught save Thyself!" May God bestow on us something of this spirit.

VI

Purgatory: The Prison House of Grace

When we speak of the "Communion of Saints" we sum up one of the most important dogmas revealed to us by our holy Catholic faith. It is at the same time one of the most comprehensive and most interesting, and, we may add, perhaps one of the least understood. It seems to say so very little, while it implies so much. It is the consequence of our redemption and sanctification, the fruit of Christ's passion and the life of grace to which we have been raised. For, by this most glorious gift of grace, purchased for us by the sufferings and death of the incarnate Son of God, we are all made members of His mystical Body, and by mutual help, mutual support, and mutual sanctification, we are meant to carry on His divine work, looking forward to the day when that work shall be made perfect and complete by the gathering together of all the elect in the kingdom of heaven. Hence, to souls bound together by this supernatural chain of faith and hope and love time is as though it were not, and real separation is impossible. Life passes away swiftly enough, and, sooner or later, death must come to all of us, but even death, to souls in grace, is but a passing change, and when we mourn for those whom it has taken from us, we "sorrow not as others, that have no hope" (1 Thes. 4:12). On the contrary, we may truly say that human affection finds in death its surest triumph, for whereas the many troubles that surround us and the weaknesses of our own frail nature must necessarily make the strongest love rejoice with trembling, death, viewed as grace would have us view it, puts an end to all these dangers, and gives to earthly love the immortality for which it craves, making it at once unchanging and eternal. "True love," says the inspired writer, "is strong as death," and therefore "many waters cannot quench it, neither can the floods drown it" (Song 8:7); it builds a bridge across that dark abyss, so terrifying to our weakness, and that bridge is the "Communion of Saints." Our God, as Jesus Christ Himself reminds us (Mark 12:27), is not the God of the dead but of the living, and therefore those of His creatures who die in grace are never dead to Him. Underneath them are the everlasting arms, as surely as they are beneath us, and in this firm faith the loneliest soul can always find abundant light and consolation. The task before us is to contemplate this life of grace in the world to come, to see and understand, as far as possible, all that our faith can tell us of the dead who die in the Lord, and therefore are so truly blessed (Rev. 14:13).

Our thoughts go up at once to that great multitude which no man can number, standing before the throne with palms in their hands, forever reigning with Christ on high (Rev. 7:9), but even as that glorious vision seems to pass before our minds, the consciousness of sin and imperfection strikes us down and bids us realize our deep unworthiness. He who tells us of that white-robed multitude tells us also (Rev. 14:5) they are *sine macula*, spotless and unstained, and therefore we must first of all direct our thoughts towards that other world revealed to us by faith and reason as the dwelling place of all those souls, who, though God's friends, are yet unworthy of a place amongst His saints. We call it Purgatory, and we speak of those abiding there as the souls of the faithful departed. We could not justly claim to be the children of the Church, were we unmindful of those for whom the Church is so solicitous. She never forgets them. Morning by morning the sacrifice of Calvary is renewed in her midst; morning by morning the divine Victim is offered up on her altars, and following closely on the loving welcome with which she greets His sacramental presence is a prayer of supplication for the dead. *Memento Domine*—"Be mindful, O Lord, of Thy servants who have gone before us." It is an indication of the spirit she would foster in our hearts, for the same thought concludes all her prayers. "May the divine assistance remain always with us," she says, "and may the souls of the faithful departed, through the mercy of God, rest in peace."

We believe then, as Catholics, that there exists a place of waiting, a place therefore of trial and most keen suffering, created by an infinitely wise and loving God for such souls as depart out of this life in a state of grace, but yet in some way debtors to His justice. It is a dogma of our faith, which hardly seems to stand in need of proof, so strongly does it appeal to reason and conscience, so manifestly does it fit in with all we know of God. If we believe that heaven is the home of absolute purity and perfection, and that nothing which is in any way defiled can pass its gates, if we believe hell to be the prison house of those who die in grievous sin, rejecting God's most patient love and hating Him until the last, we must admit the existence of a middle state for those who are not pure enough to see God face to face, and yet have not deserved eternal banishment from Him. To deny this consequence would be to lower our idea of heaven, until it ceased to be a motive for our hopes and longings, or to create a hell so cruelly unjust as to be unreasonable and impossible. Even the heathens could not be so foolish, and Plato graphically describes a future state of punishment for those who have done evil, where some must suffer hopelessly because so hopelessly corrupted, but where others, on the contrary, find a real good in what they have to undergo, since by it they are freed from all their stains.[1] It would surely therefore be a matter for astonishment were we not to find some traces of this same belief amongst the Jews, but, instead of traces only, we have the dogma put before us in its fullness, by no less an authority than the inspired word of God. In the Book of the Maccabees we read how Judas sent an offering to Jerusalem that sacrifices might be offered for the souls of the soldiers who had fallen in battle, since "it is a holy and wholesome thought to pray for the dead, that they may be freed from sins" (2 Macc. 12:46). Yet it was not until the so-called reformers of the sixteenth century had ventured to assail this well-nigh universal belief that the Church confirmed it by a solemn definition and declared it to be the divinely revealed dogma of our faith.[2]

But if, as we have said, it is a doctrine which in every way accords with what we know of human nature, its weaknesses and capabilities, not the less does it accord with what we know of God. Without it, faith in God would be impossible. True, there are many who profess belief in God and yet deny this doctrine, but a little thought would show us that their

1. *Phaedo*, 113d–114c.
2. Council of Trent, Session VI, ch. 16, Canon 30.; and Session XXII, ch. 9, Canon 3.

God is not the infinitely perfect Being who is our last end, but a counterfeit deity formed and fashioned by their own poor darkened minds. Infinite perfection implies the possession of all perfections in an infinite degree. God is therefore just, and His justice is infinite; yet at the same time He is merciful, and His mercy is equally limitless. But because He is infinitely just, He must necessarily banish from His presence any creature in whom His all-seeing eye discerns the faintest shadow of an imperfection, and because He is infinitely merciful, He is ready to forgive the worst of sinners. How can we reconcile these two most glorious attributes of God except by Purgatory? Think what sin is and what are its consequences. Broadly speaking, sin is the aversion of the will from God,[3] and the immediate consequences of this are twofold, for it inflicts a stain upon the soul, and at the same time makes it a debtor to God's justice. The soul of man is pleasing in God's sight because of the bright, shining light of reason, and that glorious participation of the divine light which we call grace; but when man's will consents to sin, it violates the order of right reason as well as the order of grace, and withdrawing itself as it were from these refulgent sources of brightness and spiritual loveliness, it buries itself in what is vile and earthly, and so incurs the stain of sin.[4] Moreover, by that same act it violates the order of divine justice, and thereby lays itself under the obligation of restitution by making itself God's debtor. In other words, the unlawful self-indulgence, which we call sin, must be expiated by voluntary or involuntary punishment, and this holds good even when the stain of sin may have been blotted out by sorrow and repentance and the

3. *ST* I, q. 94, a. 1.
4. *ST* I-II, q. 16, aa. 1 and 2.

return of the will to God. So David sinned, and repented of his sin on hearing Nathan's parable. "I have sinned against the Lord," he cried; and Nathan said: "The Lord has taken away thy sin" (2 Sam. 12:13). But though the sin was forgiven, atonement had to be made, and a heavy punishment was inflicted. How many there are like David, who may have sinned grievously, and like him also have wept bitter tears for their sin, crying out with him in the anguish of a truly contrite heart: *Peccatum meum contra me est semper*—"My sin is always before me"—and this although many years may have passed away since that dark hour when first they fell from grace. For who can measure the debt incurred by such a fall, quite apart from all those constantly recurring minor faults and sinful inclinations which are its miserable fruits? And how will such souls stand when death comes to weigh them in the scale of the awful exacting justice of Almighty God? Then there are others who, though perhaps they never have rejected God so utterly, have nevertheless learned by sad experience the weakness of our human nature in those daily falls and imperfections of which we think so little, but of which God necessarily thinks so much, and who may perhaps have suddenly been called away, without a moment for repentance. How must God treat them? If we except the little child who passes from this world in all the beauty of unsullied innocence, or the brave martyr who pours out his blood in one supreme and generous sacrifice, what must be the state of nearly every soul that quits this life in friendship and union with its Maker? It stands before His judgment seat, and for the first time realizes justice which is infinite. It sees the many follies of its life on earth, the countless faults and imperfections for which it never even grieved, the many others, sorrowed for it may be, and yet not fully expiated, the divine likeness in its being, which is its only claim to glory, so miserably disfigured and defaced—what fate could it expect save instant and eternal banishment, were justice only to be heard? But mercy speaks as well, for in all God's works, says the Angelic Doctor,[5] mercy and truth go hand in hand; or, as the inspired writer expresses it: "Mercy and truth are met together, justice and peace have kissed each other" (Ps. 85:10). The soul passes from this world into the world of Purgatory, its stains are burnt away, its debts are fully paid, and the beauty of God's image is marvelously restored.[6] Truly we have here a wonderful revelation of God and His attributes, and it was no exaggeration to say that without this dogma of our faith, belief in God would seem impossible. For not only does the teaching of the Church on this point reconcile these two grand attributes apparently so contradictory, but it goes further, and explains them in the fullest way. We have already considered the light it throws upon God's justice, and its dealing with us, but as a revelation of God's mercy it is so wonderful that we may look upon it as its very masterpiece. For when we contemplate the world in which we live, and see and note the well-nigh universal triumph of the powers of evil, when, day by day, in a thousand different ways we are brought face to face with moral failure, and so realize though ever so faintly the utter forgetfulness of God in which the vast majority of His creatures seem to live, the sight of all this, the knowledge of all this, would surely extinguish our faith in God as the Almighty Ruler, our hope in Him as the Savior of mankind, our love of Him as a most tender Father, were it not for this creation of His mercy, where justice and

5. *ST* I, q. 21, a. 4.

6. *ST* III, Supplement, Appendix I, q. 1, a, 1.

mercy are so wonderfully blended. Purgatory is the solution of this most terrifying mystery. There God wins back all that He seemed to lose in life, and the many defeats of time are more than compensated for by the great victory of eternity. There must be millions of souls who during life have wandered far from God, and yet have ever kept alive that little twinkling light of faith and reason which, even at the last hour, can show them how to find Him once again, and what we call a death-bed repentance, though always a miracle of mercy, must be a frequent source of joy to the angels of God. An old English writer expresses this very vividly in the well-known lines:

> Between the stirrup and the ground
> I mercy asked, I mercy found.[7]

And it would not be just to call this a mere poetic exaggeration, for all that God wants is the beginning of the great work of grace, the conversion of the will, and Purgatory will do the rest. We could not easily believe that one little act of contrition, imperfect perhaps in many ways, would have sufficient power to carry the sinner's soul into the glory of God's presence, but we can believe it strong enough to break the chains of sin, and make the soul God's friend, and then in that mysterious world where sin becomes impossible, and grace triumphant, God repairs His handiwork, and fits it for a place in His eternal kingdom. "Souls must be saved," says a spiritual writer, "and the saved multiplied, and the heavenly banquet crowded, even if the constraints of fire be needed to anneal the hastier works of grace. Therefore is

7. William Camden, *Remains concerning Britain.*

it that the vast realms of Purgatory are lighted up with the flames of vindictive love. Thus a huge amount of imperfect charity shall bring forth its thousands and its tens of thousands for heaven. Redemption shall cover the whole earth and be plentiful indeed, and the very unworthinesses and shortcomings of the creature shall only still more provoke the prodigality of the Blood of the Creator. Oh, the mercy of those cleansing fires! What could have devised them but a love that was almost beside itself for expedients?"[8] And again, appealing to the very sufferings of Purgatory as a proof of God's wondrous mercy, the same writer continues: "The extreme severity of the punishments of Purgatory is a consideration which leads the mind to contemplate the immense multitude of the saved, and of those saved with very imperfect dispositions, as the only solution of these chastisements. Purgatory goes as near to the unriddling of the riddle of the world as any one ordinance of God which can be named.... Now does it come natural to us to look at all this system, this terrible eighth sacrament of fire, which is the home of those souls whom the seven real sacraments of earth have not been allowed to purify completely—does it come natural to us to look at it all as simply a penal machinery?... Does not the view at once recommend itself to us that it was an invention of God to multiply the fruit of our Savior's passion, that it was intended for the great multitudes who die in charity with God, but in imperfect charity, and therefore that it is, as it were, the continuance of death-bed mercies beyond the grave?"[9] Let us then go down

8. Frederick Faber, *Creator and the Creature: The Wonders of Divine Love* (Baltimore: Murphy & Co., 1857), p. 284.

9. Ibid. pp. 338–39.

in spirit to that land of patient suffering, and contemplate the state of those most holy souls—holy, because incapable of sin, because so patient and resigned, because so precious in God's sight. It is quite possible, probable even, that many of them are bound to us by ties of blood and kindred, or the yet tenderer ties of love and friendship; once, perhaps, they shared the joys and sorrows of our lives, and helped us by their sympathy; for many reasons, therefore, we ought to feel compelled to do our best to find out all our faith can tell us of their state. Two things only has the Church defined in this most interesting subject, firstly, that there is a Purgatory, and secondly, that the souls therein detained are helped by our prayers and good works. This implies enough to satisfy the most anxious inquirer, and, with it as our groundwork, we may listen to what the saints and doctors of the Church can say by way of explanation.

It is quite true that, as a rule, the revelations of the saints cannot be put forward as an argument, but the teaching of St. Catherine of Genoa on this subject is so solidly theological that we may be pardoned if we quote it here. In Purgatory, she tells us, there is the extremity of suffering and the extremity of joy. The suffering is so great that no tongue can tell it, no mind can understand it, and on the other hand the joy is so abounding that there is nothing to compare with it, save the happiness of heaven. Moreover, it is a joy which is ever on the increase, as the separation between the soul and God is gradually destroyed. But this contentment does not take away the pain, for it is the retarding of love from the possession of its object which causes the pain, and the pain is greater according to the greater perfection of love, of which God has made the soul capable. Thus the souls in Purgatory have at once the greatest contentment and the greatest suffering, and the one in no way hinders the other.[10] A very little thought will show us how profoundly true and theological is this teaching. It puts before us joys and sorrows well-nigh unspeakable, and without appealing to the example of St. Paul and other saints of God, who superabounded with joy in all their tribulations, our own little experience is sufficient to convince us of the possibility of a union of the two. We will take the sorrows first, because in our minds, the idea of suffering is always uppermost when we think of Purgatory.

These holy souls suffer, and suffer most grievously. They are banished from God's presence at the very moment when for the first time they appreciate Him as He deserves. The heart of man was made for God, and God alone can satisfy its boundless power of love. In this life many things combine to lead it far astray, and make it seek elsewhere the good for which it was created, but when death comes, and, for the first time, all created things must stand aside, the soul sees the truth, and with a passionate longing craves for that union which alone can make it blessed. But there is a barrier in the way. With that first mighty act of love there comes the realization of sin, the bitterness of separation which it involves, and the anguish of that "hope deferred, which makes the heart sick" (Prov. 13:12). St. Thomas maintains[11] that this suffering is far beyond all that we can feel or imagine in this life. It is, he explains, of a twofold nature, the pain of loss, which is the postponement of the sight of God, and the pain of sense, by which we understand the punishment of fire, and in both respects, says the Angelic Doctor, the least pain of Purgatory

10. St. Catherine of Genoa, *Treatise on Purgatory*, quoted in Frederick Faber, *All for Jesus* (Baltimore: John Murphy Co., 1855), p. 391.

11. *ST* III, Supplement, Appendix I, q. 2, a. 1.

exceeds the sharpest pain we could be called on to endure in this life. For the more intensely we long for anything, the more keenly do we feel its loss; and because the longing of these holy souls for Him who is their highest good is most intense, since the time for enjoying it has come, and there is nothing to distract the mind in any way, the anguish of their disappointment is unspeakable. So also with regard to what we call the pain of sense. It is altogether dependent on, and in proportion to, our sensibility, and hence it is that mental sufferings are worse than bodily, and any pain which acts directly on the soul itself, the source and cause of all sensibility, must of necessity be the keenest pain of all. Once we understand the twofold cause of Purgatory—the loving torment of unsatisfied desire for God, and the vivid realization of the horror of sin—we need say no more about the intensity of its sufferings. Cardinal Newman most perfectly and most beautifully expresses the same teaching in his "Dream of Gerontius":

> When then—if such thy lot—thou seest thy Judge,
> The sight of Him will kindle in thy heart
> All tender, gracious, reverential thoughts.
> Thou wilt be sick with love, and yearn for Him,
> And thou wilt hate and loathe thyself, for though
> Now sinless, thou wilt feel that thou hast sinned
> As never thou didst feel, and wilt desire
> To slink away and hide thee from His sight,
> And yet will have a longing aye to dwell
> Within the beauty of His countenance.
> And these two pains, so counter and so keen,
> The longing for Him, when thou seest Him not,
> The shame of self at thought of seeing Him,
> Wilt be thy veriest, sharpest Purgatory.

So the work of expiation is gradually accomplished. How long it takes, God only knows; but with fixed unwavering patience, the holy souls endure it all, lonely, though in the midst of such a multitude, in the most intense silence, since their thoughts are not for words to utter, incapable of forgetfulness, or even of one poor solitary distraction, their whole being throbbing and pulsating with the fiery burning of a longing love, compared with which all other fire is but a painted imitation, ever waiting for the hour when suffering shall have done its cleansing work, and God's angels come to call them to their home of everlasting rest. And this leads us to the joys of Purgatory, for, as we said, it is a land where joy goes hand in hand with sorrow, and the first and most abundant source of joy is to be found in this sure hope and certain knowledge of their final deliverance. For when the waiting seems most wearisome, when the keen fire thrills them through and through with anguish, when their whole being seems upon the point of being drowned in bitterness, there sounds within their souls the music of an angel's whisper: *Confortetur cor tuum, et sustine Dominum*—"Let thy heart be comforted, and wait for the Lord." These words are the conclusion of the twenty-seventh Psalm, and seem to come as an inspired answer to the beautiful acts of hope of which the Psalm is full, so that we might almost call it the Psalm of the Holy Souls:

> The Lord is my light and my salvation,
> whom shall I fear?
> The Lord is the protector of my life,
> of whom shall I be afraid?
> My enemies that troubled me have themselves
> been weakened and are fallen.

> One thing have I asked of the Lord, this will I seek after,
> that I may dwell in the house of the Lord
> all the days of my life.
> My heart has said to Thee, my face has sought Thee,
> Thy face, O Lord, will I seek.
> Hide not Thy face from me, and turn not away
> in anger from Thy servant.
> Be Thou my helper, forsake me not,
> do not Thou despise me, O God my Savior.
> I believe that I shall see the good things of the Lord
> in the land of the living.

And oh, the flood of joy and happiness unspeakable which sweeps through these sorely tried souls at this thought: *Credo videre bona domini*—"I believe, I know, that I shall see the good things of the Lord!" The certainty of heaven! Could any suffering neutralize a joy like that? But there is another joy to be found in the sufferings themselves, because of the clear understanding the holy souls have of them, their knowledge of their work and purpose, and the loving resignation with which they accept them. They are the means ordained by God for the breaking down of the barriers sin has raised, by them they are enabled to pay back the debt they have incurred, even to the very last farthing, and hence they submit to them most willingly.[12] "When the soul, separated from the body," to quote once more St. Catherine of Genoa, "finds itself wanting in requisite purity, and sees in itself an impediment which cannot be taken away except by Purgatory, it at once throws itself into it with right good will. Nay, if it did not find this ordinance of Purgatory, aptly contrived for the

12. *ST* III, Supplement, Appendix I, q. 2, a. 2.

removal of this hindrance, there would instantly be born in it a hell far worse than Purgatory, inasmuch as it would see that because of this impediment, it could never get to God, who is its End. Wherefore, if the soul could find another Purgatory fiercer than this, in which it could the sooner get rid of this impediment it would speedily plunge itself therein, because of the impetuosity of the love it bears to God."[13] Here again we may turn to the beautiful poem of Newman above quoted, and in the exquisite lines in which he expresses the feeling of the soul at the judgment seat, we may trace once more the marvelous identity of thought between the Italian saint and the great English cardinal:

> Take me away, and, in the lowest deep,
> There let me be.
> And there, in hope, the lone night watches keep,
> Told out for me.
> There, motionless and happy in my pain,
> Lone, not forlorn,
> There will I sing my sad perpetual strain
> Until the morn.
> There will I sing and soothe my stricken breast,
> Which ne'er can cease
> To throb and pine and languish, till possess'd
> Of its sole peace!
> There will I sing my absent Lord and Love.
> Take me away,
> That sooner I may rise and go above,
> And see Him in the truth of everlasting day.

13. Quoted in Faber, *All for Jesus*, p. 387.

Each moment, as we have said, sees the sufferings lessen and the joys increase. The brightest jewel in the world, to borrow a striking comparison from St. Catherine, cannot reflect the sunlight, if it be hidden beneath a coating of impurities, but as these are cleansed away, it manifests its brightness more and more, until at last we see it in its perfect beauty. So is it with the soul in the cleansing fires of Purgatory. Its earthly stains are gradually destroyed, and when at last the work is done, God draws it to Himself, and being brought face to face with Him it is made like to Him and shines with the brightness of His glory.

Such then is the dogma of Purgatory, most beautiful, most reasonable and most consoling. For us it has a practical conclusion which we must not overlook, for the Church has also defined that these most holy souls are helped by our prayers, and we cannot refuse that help unless we are utterly wanting in generous love of our neighbor, in zeal for God's glory, and in care for our own interests. We have seen how they are suffering, and God longs to give them rest, eternal rest, and justice bars the way. Therefore He turns to us, and placing in our hands the boundless treasures of His atonement, He begs us, out of love for Him and pity for those souls, to pay their many debts. That is our share in the beautiful Communion of Saints, and its reward is something hard to put in words, though faith can well imagine it—the unending gratitude of a ransomed soul. Hush for a while the many noises and distractions of a sinful, disappointing world, and with ears quickened by faith, listen to the grand harmonious song forever going up before the throne of God from all His children, the hymn of the Communion of Saints: the voice of the Church Suffering, patient and pleading, "Have pity on me, have pity on me, at least you my friends, for the hand of the Lord has touched me"; the voice of the Church Militant tender and compassionate, "Eternal rest give unto them, O Lord, and let perpetual light shine upon them"; the voice of the Church Triumphant, ringing with gratitude and conscious power, "Vouchsafe, O Lord, for Thy name's sake, to reward with eternal life all them that have done us good."

VII

Hell: The Failure of Grace

In the nineteenth chapter of St. Luke's Gospel, the Evangelist puts before us a scene which is one of the most beautiful, most touching, and most instructive in Holy Scripture. He describes in most graphic words our Blessed Lord's last and most solemn entry into Jerusalem, the enthusiasm of the crowds that surrounded Him, the joy and gladness of His disciples, the fervor of their hosannas, the impotent envy of His enemies, and then the strange and sudden contrast—"seeing the city, He wept over it, saying: 'If thou also hadst known, and that in this thy day, the things that are to thy peace, but now they are hidden from thine eyes'" (Luke 19:41–42). It is indeed a wonderful picture, and it is likewise a striking and instructive lesson. Holy Scripture is the word of God, whose understanding is infinite and almighty, and therefore it is not surprising that He should teach us not merely by the words He speaks, or which He inspires, but also by the actions which those words describe. There is nothing extraordinary, therefore, or far-fetched, in taking the city of Jerusalem as a figure of the individual soul, and the story of God's dealings with that ungrateful city as a picture of His dealings with so many of His creatures. There is the same abundant outpouring of favors and blessings on the one side, the same ingratitude and repeated rebellion on the other, and the picture is completed by final rejection and terrible punishment when that ingratitude reaches its limit. The inspired writer tells us (Ps. 87) that the Lord loved the city of Sion above all the other dwelling places of His chosen people, and yet He caused it to be utterly destroyed and laid waste, because it had not known the time of its "visitation." So, contemplating as we are the workings of the supernatural life of grace, its progress and development, we dare not venture to pass by in silence the possibility of its utter failure and all which that implies. We must consider, and consider carefully, in the light of faith and reason, the final state of those souls who, like the city of Jerusalem, have neglected the things that were for their peace, the eternal destiny of those who obstinately refuse to acknowledge the end of their creation and to fulfill it, and who, therefore, are at last crushed down by the unutterable sorrow of knowing that it is forever hidden from their eyes. We must consider hell, the only part of God's vast creation on which the sunlight of His blessing never falls, the only kingdom in His mighty empire where grace cannot and may not rule supreme; "the land that is dark, and covered with the mist of death; a land of misery and darkness where the shadow of death and everlasting horror dwelleth" (Job 10:21–22).

It is a curious fact, and one well worthy of our close attention, that belief in hell is as universal as belief in God. St. Paul reminds us (Heb. 11:6) that faith in God, as the rewarder of our works, is an essential condition of our service of Him, but independently of this supernatural knowledge, we can discern in all people, of all ages, a more or less distinct belief in God, and in a future state of happiness and misery, the lingering remains, no doubt, of the first great revelation granted to our race.

It would be superfluous to appeal to the ancient writers of Greece and Rome; every student of the classics is familiar with their teaching. The learned writers of the East are not less definite, and even Muhammad, who surely tried his best to invent and propagate what we might call a "comfortable" religion, has nevertheless retained the dogma of eternal punishment. Those who broke away from the Church in each succeeding age of its existence never based the motive of their separation and revolt on this stern truth; it seems to have been reserved to our own age, so full of pride and independence, so greedy of indulgence and every sort of pleasure, to put itself in opposition to the universal feeling of past ages, and deny not merely the existence but the very possibility of what we call hell. In deference therefore to the age in which we live, we may begin by seeing what our reason ought to tell us on this subject, and how far its light can lead us in such an all-important controversy. Faith and reason never can oppose each other. That is a truth we often find ourselves forgetting, when specious arguments plunge the mind in darkness; to qualify a dogma of the faith as "unreasonable" is a gross misuse of terms, as well as a proclamation of our own ignorance. Faith and reason, as we tried to show in the first chapter, are given to us by God to help us in our search for Him; if they seem to be in opposition, and to impede our progress, the fault is ours, not God's! To quote once more the teaching of the Vatican Council on this point: "God cannot contradict Himself, nor can truth ever be opposed to truth. Whenever there appears to be a sort of contradiction, it is because the dogmas of the faith have not been rightly understood and perfectly explained, or else because the assertions of opinions are taken for dictates of reason."[1] What then does our reason tell us about eternal punishment?

Without plunging into metaphysics, or indulging in digressions to explain the nature of good and evil in the moral order, we can all admit that they are two opposing forces, working, so to speak, in opposite directions. The difference which divides them is something more than accidental, it is rather what we call essential! To use an ordinary comparison, however poor and inadequate, they run on lines which from the first diverge, and are not merely parallel, much less converging. It would seem to follow, therefore, that as long as good is good, and evil, evil, they never can produce the same result, or arrive at the same term, no matter how indefinitely the lines may be prolonged. St. Paul's comparison of the wild olive (Rom. 11:2) is strongly to the point, for the wild olive remains useless as long as it is the wild olive. But if, as the apostle says, a branch cut from the wild olive be grafted on a good tree, then it will bring forth fruit because it is a wild olive no longer. Hence our Blessed Lord Himself so pertinently asks: "Do men gather grapes of thorns, or figs of thistles?" (Matt. 7:16) But if you do away with the eternity of hell, you must infer that you do expect to find grapes growing on thorns, and figs on thistles, for you infer that good and evil, sooner or later, produce the same effect, and therefore that the difference between them is but accidental, or, in other words, that their nature is essentially the same! What appalling consequences such

1. First Vatican Council, Session III, ch. 4.

teaching would produce if really believed! It would not matter whether we formed our lives after the example of Nero or St. John, Jezebel or the Immaculate Mother of God, the end eventually would be the same! Could anything more absurd be imagined? But there is another consideration. Belief in God, as we said in a former chapter, necessarily implies belief in God's almighty power. He is the supreme and absolute Master of all the works of His hands, and possesses an unquestionable right to their dutiful service. But in His superabounding goodness, He has bestowed on man the power of free will, enabling him to give, or to refuse this service as he chooses, and a deliberate refusal on the part of man is what we call sin. Sin is therefore literally and truly war between the creature and the Almighty Creator, but it is a war which can have only one possible result. The final victory must lie with God. Of course there is the victory of grace, which means the absolute submission and repentance of the sinner, but we must put that aside for the present. Our argument here supposes deliberate rebellion, deliberately and willfully and obstinately persevered in until the last. That such folly is possible is necessarily implied by the possession of free will, and it equally implies as a logical consequence the possibility of eternal banishment from God. History records the despairing cry of Julian the Apostate as he fell in battle: "Galilaean! Thou hast conquered!" But were there no eternal hell, he might have hurled a last defiance at his Maker, and then endured with patience all the torments which the Galilaean could inflict, triumphing in the consciousness that one day they would end, and that, in reality, he would be the final conqueror.

Now we may go a little further and listen to the arguments of faith, and here as elsewhere the greatest of the

Church's theologians shall be our guide. According to St. Thomas,[2] sin is an "inordinate act," because it is a violation of the right order of things, and therefore in addition to the stain which it inflicts upon the soul, it makes it a debtor to the law so violated; and as long as this perversion continues, as long as the right order of things is being disturbed by the sinner, so long is he justly deserving of punishment. In some cases, this disturbance is only transient, whereas in others it is irreparable. If the earthquake only breaks the windows or topples down the chimneys, the damage can be easily repaired, and the house remains as good as ever; but if the foundations are thoroughly shaken and undermined, the building can no longer be considered safe or habitable, and had better be destroyed at once. In other words, says St. Thomas, if the defect be of such a nature as to destroy the very principle or foundation, then the harm is irreparable; but if, on the contrary, the principle remains untouched, it is always able to repair and make good all other injuries. For example, if owing to disease or any other cause a man's eyes have to be removed, or if the optic nerve be utterly destroyed, the blindness which results is quite incurable; but if he suffers from cataract or some other minor malformation, the blindness is but temporary, and may be done away with by proper care and nursing, or a successful operation. In the one case the very principle of vision is destroyed, in the other its working is but hindered for a time. To apply this then to the act of sin: if it be of such a nature as to utterly subvert the principle of that relationship which ought to bind our souls to God, and which consists in cleaving to Him as our first beginning and last end, or, in other words,

2. *ST* I-II, q. 87, a. 1.

the state of grace, then is its effect eternal, and the injury inflicted on the soul irreparable, though not of course beyond the healing power of God. But the rupture of that bond of love which is our only means of union with God is just what theologians mean by mortal sin; and hence, concludes St. Thomas, whatever sins so turn the soul from God as to destroy the bond of charity, incur a debt of everlasting punishment. We might almost venture, therefore, to define hell as the state of mortal sin, made eternal and indelible by the sinner's own deliberate act, and fully realized by him. "God," says Father de Ravignan, "has no need of changing anything in the state of the sinner's soul in order to punish him. He abandons him to his sin, and in that the reprobate finds his everlasting hell." It is a thought the importance of which cannot be overestimated. We are so apt to appeal to our imagination in this matter instead of to our reason, and so we imagine eternal punishment as a sort of unending penal servitude, a terrible expiation exacted by vindictive justice for crimes over and gone long ago, when in reality it is nothing of the kind. It is rather the perpetual accompaniment of the conscious malice of deliberate rebellion, eternally persisted in, and eternally realized as hopeless and unreasonable. An old legend represents the devil as reproaching God with never having offered him a chance of repentance after his fall, and there is a world of truth in God's reply, legend only though it be: "Have you ever asked for it?" So also with the reprobate soul. "It is not God who is angry," says Bishop Hedley, speaking of a soul in hell; "it is the sinner who places a barrier between himself and that Being who alone is his happiness. The sinner therefore damns himself. A soul in mortal sin only requires the dissolution of its mortal frame to be by that very fact in hell." It might perhaps be objected that it is very hard to understand how the mere fact of death, "the dissolution of this mortal frame," can effect that tremendous difference which the Catholic faith supposes to exist between the comparative happiness of a sinful life on earth, and the misery of life in hell; and the difficulty is not unreasonable, though a very little thought should be able to explain it. Grievous sin implies the loss of God, and the loss of God is hell; but as long as life lasts the soul may obstinately refuse to realize its miserable destitution, and endeavor with some show of success to make up for the loss of God by the use, or rather the abuse, of God's gifts. The varied picture of the world around us, the many joys of life, the pleasures of sense, and those still higher intellectual pleasures which gratify the mind, the society of friends and relations—all these things are tokens of God's goodness, gifts from the Giver of all good gifts, most wonderfully designed to lead us on to Him if rightly used, but by their very excellence and variety quite capable of attracting and enslaving the hearts and wills of those who use them for themselves and their own gratification, and not in obedience to God's law. But death puts an end to the delusion. When the soul of the sinner goes forth from its earthly tabernacle, it loses in an instant all that made existence pleasant, or even bearable, and what does it receive in exchange? Nothing! God ought to be all in all, for it was made for Him; but it has deliberately rejected God, and must now fall back upon itself, only to feel every faculty burning with the agony of desires that can never be gratified. It is this very truth which Cardinal Newman, in *Callista*, puts as an argument in the mouth of St. Cyprian, in order to bring home to the heathen mind of the heroine the possibility of everlasting punishment: he makes the bishop say:

Perhaps you will tell me that after death, you will cease to be. I don't believe you think so. I may take for granted that you think with me, and with the multitude of men, that you will still live and that you will still be *you.* You will still be the same being, but deprived of those outward stays and reliefs and solaces which, such as they are, you now enjoy. You will be yourself shut up in yourself. If then, on passing hence, you are cut off from what you had here, and have only the company of yourself, I think your burden will be so far greater, not less, than it is now. Suppose, for instance, you had still your love of conversing, and could not converse; your love of the poets of your race, and no means of recalling them; your love of music, and no instrument to play upon; your love of knowledge, and nothing to learn; your desire of sympathy, and no one to love; would not that be still greater misery? Let me proceed a step further. Supposing you were among those you actually did not love; supposing you did not like them, nor their occupations, and could not understand their aims; suppose there be, as Christians say, one Almighty God, and you did not like Him, and had no taste for thinking of Him, and no interest in what He was and what He did; and supposing you found that there was nothing else anywhere but He, whom you did not love and whom you wished away, would you not be still more wretched? And if this went on forever, would you not be in great inexpressible pain forever? Assuming then, first, that the soul ever needs external objects to rest upon; next, that it has no prospect of any such when it leaves this visible scene; and thirdly,

> that the hunger and thirst, the gnawing of the heart, where it occurs, is as keen and piercing as a flame; it will follow there is nothing irrational in the notion of an eternal Tartarus.[3]

Nothing irrational! The unreasonableness is surely on the side of those who refuse to realize this, and who vainly try to silence the understanding by the murmurs of an unregulated imagination and the protestations of a sickly sentimentalism. For Catholics, at all events, the existence of a place of eternal punishment is a dogma of faith, and we profess our sincere belief in it in the concluding words of the Athanasian Creed: "They that have done good shall go into everlasting life, but they that have done evil into everlasting punishment."

Having seen, therefore, how reason and faith are united in obliging us to admit this stern truth, the existence of a place of punishment which we call "hell," set apart for souls who persist in rebellion against God, and who, therefore, die in a state of grievous sin, we may now look at the subject more closely and endeavor to gather from the teaching of our faith some idea of the nature of eternal punishment. The genius of Dante sums it all up in that terrible inscription which his imagination saw emblazoned on the gates of hell:

> Through me you pass into the city of woe,
> Through me you pass into eternal pain,

---

3. John Henry Newman, *Callista* (London: Longmans, Green, and Co., 1901), ch. xix. Note: The 1900 edition of this text, *Conferences on the Life of Grace* (Kegan Paul, Trench, Trübner & Co.), gives a misspelling in the last line of the quotation from *Callista*: "external Tartarus" rather than "eternal Tartarus." This misspelling has been remedied here.

Through me among the people lost for aye.
Justice the Founder of my fabric moved,
To rear me was the task of power divine,
Supremest wisdom and primaeval love.
Before me things create were none, save things
Eternal, and eternal I endure!
All hope abandon, ye who enter here![4]

But we have no need of poets, even though they be as great and as truly theological as Dante, to help us to put in words the nature of eternal punishment. From the many pages in Sacred Scripture, in which this truth is plainly put before us, we need only turn to one, in which our Blessed Lord Himself describes the day of judgment, and with His own sacred lips formulates the final sentence which He will pass upon the souls of the reprobate: "Depart from me, accursed, into everlasting fire" (Matt. 25:41). We need no more. These dread words of God Incarnate sum up briefly but most clearly all that we want to know. Let us do our best then to realize something of their meaning.

"All punishment," says St. Thomas,[5] "must be proportionate to the offense or sin for which it is inflicted. But in every sin we may distinguish two acts of the will, inasmuch as by sin, the soul first of all turns away from God, the unchanging, infinite Good, and in this respect is guilty of an infinite offense, and then, in the second place, chooses in place of God some transitory pleasure, an act which is finite in every way. The rejection of God is punished by the loss of

4. Dante, *Inferno*, trans. H. F. Gary (London: George Bell and Sons, 1888), III.1–9.

5. *ST* I-II, q. 87, a. 4.

God, which may be truly called infinite, since it is the deprivation of an infinite good, and the unlawful preference of the creature is expiated by the finite pain of sense." Our Blessed Lord expresses this double penalty in the words of His dread sentence: "Depart from me, into everlasting fire"—the pain of loss, and the pain of sense.

The pain of loss! We have already tried to show the origin and cause of this suffering, but a little repetition may help us to see it more clearly. Almighty God has created us for Himself, bestowing upon us a spiritual nature, which implies an instinctive longing for Him, and for the happiness which can only come by seeing Him face to face and possessing Him. During the time of this life of probation, He hides Himself behind a veil, and asks us to give Him our free service, seeing Him only by faith, possessing Him by hope and love. But when death comes, the veil is drawn aside.

The time of probation is over. The soul understands perfectly that God is her last end, and she longs for Him and desires to possess Him because the possession of Him is perfect happiness. But, as we have already said, if she be in the state of grievous sin, the love of God, which is the principal and only means of union with Him, is altogether absent; it has been willfully destroyed. The soul sees, therefore, that she never can possess God, that she has lost Him forever, and the realization of that loss is hell! The possession of God is eternal happiness, the loss of God is eternal misery; and when those awful words, "Depart from me," ring through the silence of eternity, they are to the lost soul the revelation of its hopeless fate. God is light, infinite light, uncreated light. In its mortal life the soul has enjoyed the possession of this light to a greater or less degree; now she has approached the unfailing source of it all, only to see it disappear forever, and to feel herself plunging into an intellectual darkness that will last forever.

And love has gone too! Light is the food of the understanding, and love is the food of the will, and God is light, and God is love, for He is the one object of the mind and the heart; we mean nothing else when we say that He is our last end. He Himself is the eternal home of all the souls whom He calls out of nothingness, for He made them for Himself, and, therefore, during the time of their probation in this world His voice is ever calling them: "My son, give me thy heart"; "I am thy reward, exceedingly great"; but this gracious voice no longer speaks to the reprobate. They chose their own way, they lived for themselves and not for Him, they made their home on earth and in the things of this world, only to realize too late that it has all passed like a dream, and that their heavenly home is closed against them; and with a mind crushed down by darknes, and a will broken by the greatness of its misery, though still rebellious and unrepentant, the lost soul enters on its everlasting exile. Perhaps we might as well confess at once that we cannot put in words the exceeding horror of the loss of God, because we do not appreciate Him as we ought, nor do we understand His infinite beauty and attractiveness. What a power there is in the beauty and loveliness and attractiveness of earthly things! The wanderer in a foreign land thinks of his own home and country, and because the beauty of it haunts his memory all else grows dull by comparison. The artist lives apart in a world of beauty of his own, a world of ideals it may be, and yet so real a world to him that the ordinary things of earth can hardly win a passing thought from him; and our own hearts too, do they not clothe with beauty everything to which they cling, and faces that have long since passed away still linger on unfaded in our hearts, because of the beauty which is theirs, a beauty none the less real to us because, perhaps, our own creation. Yet the beautiful as existing in the world around us, or as seen by the mind and the heart, is after all but a participation, and a feeble participation, of the unspeakable beauty of God. What then would be its power upon the soul? What the agony of its loss?

It may seem well-nigh useless to speak of the "pain of sense," seeing that it must be insignificant when compared with pain which in itself is infinite and eternal; but if, as we have said, the pain of loss would seem to be beyond our understanding because of its greatness and its purely spiritual nature, the pain of sense on the other hand appeals to us with a special force for the very opposite reason. Hence this secondary punishment, and all the suffering which it involves, is frequently put before us by the Holy Scripture in the most vivid language, and is usually expressed by the one term "fire." "Depart from me, into everlasting fire." With regard to the nature of this fire the Church has defined nothing; we are free to follow our own opinion. In the ages of faith, the common Catholic teaching maintained that the fire of hell was a real material fire, but since it is the fashion today to look askance at the theories of these old-fashioned teachers, and even to reject them as impossible in the light of our superior education, we may devote a moment to the examination of their explanations of this difficulty. It may be, after all, that they are not so foolish or unreasonable as we are tempted to think. St. Thomas shall be their spokesman; he, at least, is never foolish or unreasonable, even when cross-examined by a nineteenth-century intellect, and here as elsewhere there is a weight and grandeur in the arguments of the Angelic Doctor which must win our admiration, even if they fail to win our full assent. Great as St. Thomas was, or rather because he was so great, he had a childlike reverence for the words of Jesus Christ and His inspired servants, and, therefore, all his efforts go to show how the words of Sacred Scripture can reasonably bear a literal sense, instead of weakly yielding to the clamors of an empty so-called science, and endeavoring to explain them all away. St. Thomas teaches, therefore, that the spiritual immaterial souls really suffer from the fire of which God's word so often speaks, because it is made the instrument of divine justice, and as such binds them down and holds them fast within its fiery grasp, a penalty so utterly repugnant to their spiritual nature and its natural rights and dignity, as to cause the keenest anguish. For it is unnatural, as he says, that a spiritual being should be so imprisoned in anything material as to be cut off from all enjoyment of its natural freedom, and the torment of the penal fire is due to this power of imprisoning the soul, a power conferred on it by God as the instrument of His justice.[6] But whatever opinion we may hold as to the nature of the fire, it is surely sufficient for us that our Blessed Lord, who could not and would not exaggerate, repeatedly alludes to it as a very terrible suffering; and yet, after all, as a spiritual writer well says, once we put aside the thought of the loss of God, we are speaking of hell with the hell left out[7]; so we may pass on to consider one or two of the many objections put forward with such assurance by modern "thinkers." The objections themselves are not modern. St. Thomas discussed them and replied to them more than six centuries ago, but

6. *ST* III, Supplement, Appendix I, q. 1, a. 1.
7. Frederick Faber, *Spiritual Conferences* (London: T. Richardson, 1859), p. 396.

they reappear from time to time in a new garb and with a fresh flourish of trumpets, as though they were the special intellectual product of each particular age. They are based, as indeed are all objections against revealed truth, on a more or less voluntary misconception and misstatement of the dogma they assail, and though the manner of attack may differ, its groundwork is ever the same. They protest against the doctrine of eternal punishment because they consider it to be altogether repugnant to God's justice and God's love. It is repugnant, they say, to God's justice. St. Thomas thus formulates their objection: "No sin can deserve eternal punishment, because there must be some proportion between the punishment and the offense for which it is inflicted. But what proportion is there between the act of a moment and an eternal hell?"[8] The Angelic Doctor, in reply, points out first of all that this argument, taken literally, would be fatal to all justice, human and divine, for we constantly see crimes that were committed in a moment punished by years of imprisonment, or even death, which is the human equivalent of eternal punishment; the obvious explanation being that the proportion between the crime and its punishment is never based on the duration of the act, but on its malice and gravity. It is quite true that at first sight there seems to be a terrible disproportion between the momentary act of sin and eternal reprobation, but we have to take into account what that momentary act involves. It is not easy, and indeed it would be presumptuous, to judge of individual acts that come under our notice, but looking at the matter in the abstract, and taking mortal sin to be what we have explained it to be, the willful, deliberate, eternal rejection of God, we are

8. *ST* I-II, q. 87, a. 3, ad 1.

bound to admit that it deserves an eternal hell. For the soul that consents to such an act does so with full knowledge of the consequences. It is not taken by surprise; it has every chance. It has been sealed with the image of God, redeemed by the Blood of Christ, crowned with the most wonderful gifts and graces, and yet it deliberately refuses to listen to the dictates of its own reason, it defaces and destroys as far as it can the beauty of the divine likeness, it willfully abuses and flings away its graces and its gifts, it tramples underfoot the Blood of its Savior, and then, rebellious to the last, it passes out of this world. It has literally chosen sin for its last end, and therefore, as St. Thomas says, it has the will to sin eternally. But, it might be urged, may it not repent after death? Even Holy Scripture seems to imply this when it represents sinners in hell "repenting and groaning for anguish of spirit," and saying, "we have erred from the way of truth, and the light of justice has not shined unto us, and the sun of understanding has not risen upon us. We wearied ourselves in the way of iniquity and destruction, and have walked through hard ways, but the ways of the Lord we have not known" (Wisdom 5:3, 6–7). Is not this something very like repentance, and if so, is it altogether useless? It most certainly is useless, for the simple reason that the time for repentance has passed away. God has given us the day of this life as the time of merit, and He bids us "work while we have the day, because the night comes when no man can work" (John 9:4). If He had promised us a second chance in eternity, how should we employ the time of this life? If so many lead careless and wicked lives now, what would it be like under such conditions? Common sense obliges us to see the reasonableness of a fixed time of probation, to be followed by just rewards and punishments. But, after all, is this "repenting and groaning for anguish of spirit," which Sacred Scripture attributes to the reprobate, true and sincere repentance? Is it repentance at all? According to St. Thomas, repentance or contrition implies a sorrow of heart which is based on the love of God, inspired therefore by His grace, and meritorious in His sight.[9] But it is manifest from what we have said that however real the grief of the reprobate may be, it is certainly not prompted by the love of God. The free will of the reprobate soul is turned away from God, seeing that he loves the wickedness for which he is punished, and would indulge in it again if he could, though he hates the punishment which is its consequence.[10] His grief therefore is based on the hatred of punishment rather than on the hatred of sin. And in another place the Angelic Doctor says: "The repentance of the lost is useless, because their wills are confirmed in wickedness. They have no regret whatever for the malice of sin, but only for the punishment it has entailed; and hence, instead of suggesting any hope of forgiveness, their grief only fills them with despair."[11] Evidently then God's justice is not at fault, and so an appeal is made to His love as an argument against eternal punishment; but this objection is even more unreasonable. It is precisely because God is infinite love that there is such a place as an eternal hell. To quote Dante once more:

> To rear me was the task of Power Divine,
> Supremest Wisdom, and Primaeval Love.

9. *ST* III, Supplement, q. 1, a. 1.
10. *ST* I-II, q. 13, a. 4.
11. *ST* III, q. 86, a. 1.

Notice the words *primaeval love—prima amore*. Not love such as we know it, full of countless imperfections even at its best; but *prima amore*—the first, the best, the most perfect, most patient, most generous love: love, in fine, which is infinite and eternal, and when such a love is willfully, deliberately and persistently rejected, and rejected with contempt, it is at last withdrawn, and its absence creates an eternal hell.

The dogma of everlasting punishment is a standing rebuke to man's self-worship. It is a perpetual reminder of his littleness, his ignorance and his dependence on God, and that is why it is such a stumbling block in the way of those whose only creed seems to be the exaltation of self, the glorification of fallen humanity. It is not that they cannot believe it, the evidence for it is too convincing; but they will not, and no amount of evidence can overcome that obstacle. Our Lord Himself has said it, and as a fitting conclusion we may listen to His words:

> There was a certain rich man, who was clothed in purple and fine linen, and who feasted sumptuously every day. And there was a certain beggar named Lazarus, who lay at his gate, full of sores, desiring to be filled with the crumbs that fell from the rich man's table. But no man gave unto him; moreover, the dogs came and licked his sores. And it came to pass that the beggar died, and was carried by the angels into Abraham's bosom; the rich man also died, and he was buried in hell. And lifting up his eyes when he was in torments, he saw Abraham afar off and Lazarus in his bosom. And he cried and said: "Father Abraham, have mercy on me, and send Lazarus that he may dip the tip of his finger in water to cool my tongue, for

I am tormented in this flame." And Abraham said to him: "Son, remember that thou didst receive good things in thy lifetime, and Lazarus evil things, but now he is comforted and thou art tormented. And besides all this, between us and you there is fixed a great abyss, so that they who would pass from hence to you cannot, nor from thence come hither." And he said: "Then, Father, I beseech thee that thou wouldst send him to my father's house, for I have five brethren, that he may testify unto them, lest they also come into this place of torments." And Abraham said to him: "They have Moses and the prophets; let them hear them." But he said: "Nay, Father, but if one went to them from the dead they will do penance." And he said to him: "If they hear not Moses and the prophets, *neither will they believe if one rise again from the dead*" (Luke 16).

VIII

Heaven: The Triumph of Grace

G*ratia Dei vita aeterna!* In the last of our reflections on grace, we pointed out that the works of God, in the lives and souls of His creatures, may be looked at in two ways. We may consider them according to their pre-existence in the eternal all-seeing mind of God, as determined by His will, or we may study them as they are in themselves, in their varied order and succession, the many changes they undergo, their actions and sufferings, as they gradually develop and finally attain the purpose of their being, or fail in its accomplishment. We were then considering man's supernatural life from the former point of view, whereas, in these chapters, we have confined ourselves to the latter, since our purpose was, as we stated, "to contemplate the workings of this supernatural life, to understand the sources of its power and energy, the means to which it has recourse in times of weakness and failure, and the consequences of final triumph or defeat." By this route we have once more arrived at the term; we are once more face to face with that most glorious supernatural end for which God made us: the perfect knowledge, love, and possession of Himself! *Gratia Dei vita aeterna*—The grace of God is everlasting life!

Man has an instinctive hope of a higher and nobler life than this world can give, and the groundwork of this hope is his faith in a future state. We appealed to this universal belief when we were speaking of eternal punishment, for, as we then pointed out, it is not merely the idea of a future state, which reason puts before us, but a future state of happiness or misery, reward or punishment, according to the life we live here below. For man, as a reasonable being, gifted therefore with understanding and free will, is the master of his own acts, and deliberately chooses for himself the paths he intends to pursue. In other words, there is and must be some clear and definite end before his mind, moving him to this or that particular course of action; and it is the moral goodness or evil of the purpose he has in view which specifies his action, and stamps it as good or bad in the moral order.[1] But common sense forbids us to suppose an indefinite series of such incentives to action. There must be what we call a last end, an end in which the will of man finds all that it can desire, and to which in reality all other ends are but as means. And what is this last end? According to St. Thomas,[2] it is nothing less than perfect happiness, for nothing less than that can satisfy the heart of man; and hence it is that all men are of one accord in seeking happiness, though, as we must confess, all are not agreed as to how and where this happiness may be found. Some would have us seek it in the paths of honor and glory, or in the possession of abundant riches, and the enjoyment of the many pleasures of mind and body that

1. *ST* I-II, q. 1, a. 1.
2. *ST* I-II, q. 1, a. 7.

are their fruits; but the voice of nature is not easily silenced, and it tells us very clearly that it was not for such things as these that we came forth from nothingness, crowned with such manifold gifts. No created good can give us perfect happiness.[3] The good we seek is limitless and boundless—nothing less therefore than the source of all good, God Himself, who alone can satisfy our desire with good things (Ps. 103:5).

It surely cannot be denied that life would be a dismal failure, if this world were the end of all. Quite apart from what we learn by faith, a daily experience burns in upon the soul the knowledge of that conflict between the opposing powers of good and evil, ever waging in us and around us, and so frequently resulting in the triumph of the latter. The many so-called social problems are evidence of this. Something has gone wrong somewhere, causing suffering and sorrow as a necessary consequence, and against this all our natural instincts rise in obstinate revolt, urging us to do our best to set things right, even though we feel we know not how or where to begin. For we are convinced that suffering and injustice cannot be the normal condition of things. "It is one of the strong proofs of God's existence, and man's immortality," says Bishop Hedley, "that there lies in the heart of every human being the inextinguishable conviction or inspiration that evil cannot finally triumph."[4] We cannot believe that so many millions of our race have lived and suffered and died in vain! We cannot persuade ourselves, no matter how we try, that so many brave, enduring men and loving women have borne the burden of the day and the heat, only to rest forever

3. *ST* I-II, q. 2, a. 8.
4. Hedley, *Retreat,* p. 96.

in the grave! The very thought of it makes our hearts ache, and it would be but a poor and empty consolation to say to ourselves: "All this is fate, all this is the result of hopeless necessity and must go on forever, and the only prospect before us is the nothingness of death." It cannot be! It is against the instincts of our reason, and the dictates of our common sense, ever loudly protesting that there must come a time when virtue is rewarded and vice punished, and when justice reigns supreme. We talk about "success" and "failure" in this life, but no matter how sincerely we may wish to talk, there is deep in our hearts a strange uneasy consciousness that the words are but conventional. They might possibly change places, we cannot help thinking, if right were might, and we feel that a day will come when they may be transposed for good and all. It is this hope of better things which makes our lives worth living, and enables us to solve its puzzling riddles and endure its heavy burdens. Look at that wonderful story put before us by Holy Scripture, which by its very pathos, no less than by its moral grandeur, has become so familiar to all of us as well-nigh to have grown into a proverb, the story of Job and his sufferings. We should utterly miss its real lesson were we to imagine that it had been handed down through the long ages merely to teach us patience under trial. The heart of its teaching is disclosed to us in the magnificent profession of faith and hope uttered by an innocent man in the hour of his abasement, when sorrow and misunderstanding had crushed him to the very earth: "I know that my Redeemer lives, and that at the last day I shall rise out of the earth and be clothed again with my body, and in my flesh I shall see my God, whom I myself shall see, and my eyes shall behold, and not another: this my hope is laid up in my bosom" (Job 19:25). For our experience of life, at all events, but rarely brings us face to face with sufferings so manifold, and, of their very nature, so ennobling as those which were laid upon Him. What we see is in every way more vulgar and more commonplace, of the sort imagined so vividly and expressed so powerfully by a well-known modern writer in words which we may be allowed to quote in full:

> Thou knowest my life, O God! that I was poor, so poor, and unlovely and alone! And each day I awoke so weary that I had scarce the strength to struggle up that I might go forth to work for the day's bread. And night after night I laid me down so tired, too tired to sleep. And, as I lay, the unendurable thought of the burden which I must take up on the morrow, and every morrow, and the still more unendurable thought of dying, and being thrust down among foul and rolling things into black nothingness and decay, set my heart leaping like the heart of the hunted and desperate creature which hears the hounds behind it, but sees no nook or cranny into which to creep that it may escape their cruel fangs.[5]

But if this be a true picture of countless lives, and it most surely is, who could look upon it, and realize its utter misery, and then profess his faith in the existence of Almighty God, unless that same firm faith in God assured him that the sufferings of this life were not worthy to be compared to the glory that is to be revealed? For faith in God implies belief in a God of infinite power, infinite wisdom, and infinite love. It was this faith which nerved the heart of Job and upheld

5. Coulson Kernahan, *God and the Ant* (New York: Ward, Lock, & Bowden, 1895), p. 18.

him in his hour of tribulation; and it was this faith which enabled him to pass through the furnace of trial, seven times heated though it was; a faith, a belief, within the reach of our poor ordinary efforts also, a knowledge we possess in common with him by virtue of our common humanity. Once again then, as ever, we see our faith and reason walking hand in hand, showing us the same truth, enforcing the same lesson, for while reason so unfalteringly asserts the existence of another life beyond the grave, in which its natural instincts place all that is good and beautiful and true, faith stands by its side to help it and confirm it, by declaring that the good and true and beautiful for which we long is in reality infinite in perfection, being none other than the Goodness, Truth, and Beauty of the infinite God Himself. This is the great truth we have now to examine, the nature of that "heaven," placed before us by divine revelation, when it bids us ever to incline our hearts to keep God's justifications, "because of the reward." What then do we mean by heaven, and what does our faith teach us about it?

Heaven is the beautiful dwelling place of the Sacred Humanity of Jesus, the everlasting home prepared from before the foundation of the world for those of God's creatures who should be found worthy of a share in its blessedness. Its gates were first thrown open when the trial of the angels was accomplished and the light of the vision of God burst upon the intelligences of those who had persevered. But they, like God Himself, were purely spiritual, and therefore we may say that it was not until our Blessed Lord ascended from the Mount of Olives and enthroned His human nature at the right hand of the Father, that heaven became, as He Himself described it, and as we now love to think of it, the many mansions of our Father's house. Where in the mighty universe this land of happiness may lie we do not know, for God has not revealed it to us; but it would be a great mistake to hastily conclude that therefore we know nothing, and that all that we can say is purely fanciful. Though, for His own good reasons, God has left us ignorant as to *where* it is, He tells us clearly *what* it is, and from the high mountain of revealed truth, as from another Nebo, we can see the promised land; and no matter how many years of wandering in the desert lie before us, we can, whenever we wish, refresh our wearied hearts and spur on our lagging footsteps, by turning our eyes towards that world of happiness where God will be all in all.

The very first truth impressed upon the minds of her children by the Catholic Church is that God has created us in His own likeness, marking our souls with the seal of His own adorable image that we might know and understand the purpose of our creation, that we might realize our own great task of living for Him and for His glory, and so give back to God the things that are God's. It is in this likeness or resemblance to its Creator that the perfection of the rational creature consists, being gradually worked out and developed in this life and only finished and completed when the veil is drawn aside and the soul sees its Maker face to face. "When He shall appear," says the apostle, "we shall be like unto Him, because we shall see Him as He is" (1 John 3:2).

For this resemblance to God consists in knowing Him and loving Him, according to our limited capabilities, as He knows and loves Himself; and hence we see at once that it can only be found in the intellectual part of our nature, since it is only by means of our intellectual powers that we are capable of knowledge and love. But for the sake of clearness, we may distinguish in it three grades of intensity. All men are capable of knowing and loving their Creator, because all possess the same human nature, made up of a body and a reasonable soul, and this aptitude or capability constitutes the first grade, which St. Thomas justly calls the likeness of "nature." But many souls have more. In them the divine resemblance deepens into what the Angelic Doctor calls the likeness of "grace," and this consists, as we have seen in previous chapters, in that habitual union with God which supposes and is based upon the more or less intimate knowledge and love existing in souls made beautiful by faith, hope, and charity. In this world, however, for many obvious reasons, it cannot attain its full perfection, and hence there remains the likeness of "glory," which is to be the reward of God's servants in the life to come.[6] We want to see the full significance of this and the manner of its accomplishment.

We said that this likeness of the soul to God was the groundwork of its perfection, and that it was to be found in the intellectual powers of the soul. This is equally the case whether we are speaking of the likeness of nature or the likeness of grace; and it is a truth which we learned in the pages of our Catechism, when we were taught to recognize the divine likeness in our soul in its triple power of understanding, memory, and will. But because glory, like grace, far from destroying nature, really and truly perfects it, we must apply the same teaching to the life of the soul in the world to come, and we shall find that the ultimate perfection which it there attains consists in the perfection of these same intellectual powers, for there God Himself gives to the understanding the fullness of light, the fullness of peace to the will and to the memory the fullness of eternity.

6. *ST* I, q. 93, a. 4.

In heaven God will be to the mind the fullness of light. What do we mean by this? "While we are in the body," says St. Paul, "we are pilgrims from the Lord." We are separated from Him who is our last end, exiles from our Father's house, wanderers in a foreign land. This is a truth borne in upon us by the beautiful things of this world which surround us on every side, no less than by the many sorrows and miseries of which we were just now speaking. For when God made the world, He blessed it, because He saw that it was good; and though man's sin provoked His curse and covered the earth with the thorns and briars of suffering, yet it was not wholly spoiled. It is not all sorrow and misery. To quote once more the eloquent writer already referred to: "Who of us can truly say of our lives that the evil was greater than the good? That the gladness was less than the grief? For every tear that starts to the eye our lips have worn a thousand smiles. Love and friendship, and little children, fields and flowers, sea and sky, sunshine and starlight, have made life glad and beautiful."[7] But all these things are meant to lead us on to God. By their very beauty, their varied perfections, their attractiveness, they speak to us of Him who formed and fashioned them, and gave them to us, the divine, almighty Artist, the tender Father, whose goodness and beauty they so faintly shadow forth. Sadness and sorrow and the many wearinesses of life drive us to God; the joys and pleasures of earth are meant to draw us to Him. We cannot rest in them, even if we try, for we were not made for them, beautiful as they may be, but for Him who is reflected in them. Hence St. Paul says so justly that we see God now as in a looking glass, and that cannot satisfy us, nor shall we ever be satisfied until His glory shall

7. Kernahan, *God and the Ant*, p. 25.

appear and we stand face to face with the Creator of all, for in that clear vision of Him, and in that alone, can we find perfect happiness. To prove this same great truth, St. Thomas lays down two most certain principles. "Man," he says, "is never perfectly happy as long as one unsatisfied desire remains within his soul, and then, in the next place, the perfection of every faculty is always in proportion to its attainment of its object." From these two principles the Angelic Doctor concludes that man's ultimate and perfect happiness can be nothing less than the unclouded vision of God, for, he argues, if our intellect be cognizant of some effect, without knowing anything of its cause beyond its mere existence, it must necessarily desire a fuller knowledge and endeavor to obtain it, since its perfection depends upon the completeness with which it apprehends its object. Hence to know the created things around us, and yet to know nothing of their Creator save the bare fact of His existence, would make real happiness impossible. The mind demands and necessarily requires a full and perfect knowledge of the first great cause, and in this knowledge of its Maker and the union with Him which it implies, finds perfect happiness.[8] This, and nothing less than this, is the attainment of its last end, the satisfaction of all its desires, and therefore theologians call it the "Beatific Vision," or the sight that makes us happy.

It may seem at first sight that we are no nearer than when we began, and that we are attempting to explain what is in reality totally beyond us. We talk about the "Beatific Vision," but the words hardly convey any definite idea to our minds. As far as this life is concerned, we are met by the words of Sacred Scripture assuring us that "no man has seen God at

8. *ST* I-II, q. 3, a. 8.

any time," and we cannot forget that most striking scene in the Book of Exodus, where Moses, the chosen friend and servant of God, buoyed up by the wonderful condescensions of his Maker, pleaded and entreated for this very grace. "If I have favor in Thy sight, show me Thy face, show me Thy glory." And God replied: "Thou canst not see my face, for no man can see me and live. But when my glory shall pass, I will set thee in a cleft of the rock, and protect thee with my right hand until I pass, and I will take away my hand, and thou shall see my back, but my face thou canst not see" (Ex. 33:13, 19–20). St. Paul too was caught up into what he calls the third heaven, and he tells us that what he saw may not be put in words, and that over and above there was something which eye has never seen, nor ear heard, nor heart of man imagined. Truly it would seem that the silence of prayer was more fitted for such a subject than the heaping together of words, and yet our faith falters not nor trembles, but contemplates the revealed truths of God, and shows us clearly and definitely the happiness of our heavenly home.

The "Beatific Vision," then, which makes heaven what it is, is nothing less than the sight of God face to face; that is to say, it is an intellectual act by which the soul attains its last end, and, having attained it, is filled with the joy of possessing it[9]; and our Blessed Lord Himself would seem to impress this wonderful truth upon us when He asserts so solemnly: "This is eternal life, to know Thee, the true God" (John 17:3). In this life we know God by faith; but in eternity, when "that which is perfect is come, that which is in part shall be done away" (1 Cor. 13:10), and "the glory of the Lord shall be revealed" (Rom. 8:18). When we were speak-

9. *ST* I-II, q. 3, a. 4.

ing of faith we showed that, since all supernatural truth is of its very nature far beyond the reach of a created mind unless its natural powers be supplemented by divine assistance, it was necessary that God should give to the mind that supernatural help we call the light of faith—a light because it manifests—a light of faith because the truths so manifested put forward no intrinsic evidence. But in heaven all is changed. The veils that tried us so much in this life are drawn aside, the deepest mysteries are made clear, they flood the mind with the brightness of their evidence, and faith is lost in knowledge. Yet human nature is not changed. Its powers are ever finite, and God is infinite, and therefore, in the place of faith, another supernatural help is given which we call the light of glory. By this most wonderful gift the mind of man is lifted up and strengthened, and so endowed with power from on high, that the poor trembling soul may gaze upon the unveiled glory of God, the eternal fountain of all life and all knowledge, hitherto hidden in light unapproachable, and man sees God and lives!

But we cannot know God and see His infinite perfections without instantly cleaving to Him, and preferring Him above all things, and hence the immediate consequence of the vision of God is an unending act of love. To see God face to face and not love Him would be as impossible as to pass into a glowing furnace and not feel the heat. In this life it is very different. By the fall of our first parents, not to speak of our own repeated falls, our wills have become weakened, and a sad experience teaches us that though our conscience may tell us what is right, our poor weak wills may turn to what is wrong, and as long as life lasts, so long will this struggle continue, and always shall we lean to sin and evil, and always shall we shrink from duty and from good. But the vision of God will change all this, and God will be to the will the fullness of peace. The instant that the light of God's countenance is signed upon us, our wills are made perfect, and forsaking forever all that is unworthy of them, they cleave at once and forever to the good that is eternal. Our freedom is not destroyed, but rather made complete and perfect, and what God wills, as He wills it, and because He wills it, becomes the delight of the soul. Moreover, in the light of the Beatific Vision the soul sees the love of God for His creatures, and the sight and perfect knowledge of that love, unutterable and eternal, at once wins back such a return of love, that her strong immortal life would break with its intensity, were such a thing possible, when the vision is even then confirming her in her immortality. To know God, to love God, to possess God, her gratitude is summed up and expressed in that inspired cry of the Psalmist: "Thou art the God of my heart, and the God that is my portion forever" (Ps. 73:26). Forever! God will be to the memory the fullness of eternity! The soul sees that God's love will never change, that it cannot change. It cannot change, because such a privation would be a punishment which an all-just God could never inflict except because of sin, and sin is impossible to the soul that has once gazed on the beauty of the all-beautiful God. Its happiness is therefore eternal. The soul sees that she can never fall away from God; she sees that God can never abandon her, and so her joy is made full and will endure forever. Millions and millions of ages will pass in that beautiful kingdom of light, but they can bring no cloud to the bright sunshine of that joy. And it is a joy which never palls, a happiness which never wearies. The soul is never used to it, never tired of it, never loses anything of its first unspeakable delight. The rapture of the first moment endures for all eternity, as long as God shall be God.

But this is not all! A day must come when the body and soul are once more united, and we profess our firm faith in this truth and our longing hope for it in the closing words of the Creed: "I believe in the resurrection of the body, and life everlasting." It was this same faith and hope which supported Job, as we have already pointed out. "I know that my Redeemer lives, and that at the last day I shall rise out of the earth and be clothed again with my body, and in my flesh I shall see my God, this my hope is laid up in my bosom." The effects of the vision of God on the soul overflow on the body, and confer upon it also the most wonderful gifts, so wonderful as to appear almost a new nature. St. Paul describes them to us: "It is sown in corruption, it shall rise in incorruption; it is sown in dishonor, it shall rise in glory; it is sown in weakness, it shall rise in power; it is sown a natural body, it shall rise a spiritual body" (1 Cor. 15:42, 44). Let us see what these gifts imply. While we live in this world we are under the law of suffering, for our bodies are corruptible of their very nature, and a day must come when the health and strength of which we are sometimes so proud must forsake us utterly, and we shall die. "The dust returns to the earth from whence it came, and the spirit returns to God who gave it" (Eccles. 12:7). "But when the time of reunion comes, when the trumpet sounds and the dead rise again, we shall be changed. For this corruptible must put on incorruption, and this mortal must put on immortality; and when this mortal has put on immortality then shall come to pass the saying that is written: Death is swallowed up in victory! O Death, where is thy victory? O Death, where is thy sting?" (1 Cor. 15:52–55)

The second gift of which St. Paul speaks is that of brightness or "glory." "It is sown in dishonor, it shall rise in glory." When our Savior on the mountaintop allowed the glory which was in His soul to transfigure His mortal body, we are told that His face shone like the sun, and His garments became white as snow, and He Himself has assured us that, in like manner, the bodies of the just shall "shine as the sun in the kingdom of their Father" (Matt. 13:43). But brightness and beauty imply a further gift: "It is sown in weakness, it shall rise in power." There may be some few people in this world whose lines of life have fallen in pleasant places, and who hardly know the meaning of incessant hard work and its consequent weariness; but for the great majority of our race, the hewers of wood and drawers of water, whose life from morning till night is one long round of toil, what comfort and consolation in this thought! "It is sown in weakness, it shall rise in power." To go where we will, to do what we like, as though we shared in some mysterious way in God's omnipotence and immensity, and yet never to feel the burden of fatigue or the lassitude that spoils the most enthralling pleasure. And then, lastly, "it is sown a natural body, it shall rise a spiritual body." When our Lord rose from the dead, there was no need to roll away the stone that covered the mouth of the tomb. His glorified body passed through it as the rays of the sun pass through the clear crystal. So also when the disciples had closed and barred the doors of the upper room, for fear of the Jews, Jesus came and stood in the midst of them, and it was His own real self and not a mere phantom. "Touch me, and see," He said, "it is I myself. A spirit has not flesh and bones as I have"; and this gift also is bestowed on those who have won for themselves a place in the kingdom of God.

There are many other thoughts over which we might linger, for the subject is and ought to be attractive to those who are looking forward to the coming of this kingdom, even as homesick exiles love to think about the beauties of their fatherland. The endowment of the glorified bodies of the just with these gifts revealed to us by St. Paul necessarily implies powers of enjoyment which we can hardly imagine. The pleasures of sense here in this world are innocent in themselves and in no way against God's law. But they sometimes seem to be the means of making us forget God's law, because of their strange power. They intoxicate the mind and heart, and even seem to dominate free will itself. In heaven they will exist in all their intensity, and to surrender ourselves to their uttermost delights will be an act of highest worship and perfection. Then there is the joy which arises from the company of the blessed. Love is the best, most perfect, most absorbing of all earthly joys and at the same time the most God-like, for "God is love." What must be the bliss of a life—an unending life—amongst unnumbered millions of perfect beings, loving each one of them, and being loved in return with a love surpassing all possibilities of earthly love. Yet we do not love, nor are we loved by all alike! The natural affections of earth are not extinguished by the happiness of heaven. On the contrary they are intensified in every way, and what a joy to be with those we loved so dearly when on earth and to realize that another separation is impossible. The partings of earth are bitter, and sometimes cast a shadow on the soul which never seems to lift, but the deeper the shadow and the more complete our loneliness, the brighter is our gladness and our joy when once again we meet those whom we have lost:

> Pouring the might of love from soul to soul
> In the untold communion of the blest!

Forever and forever we shall dwell with them amongst that multitude that no man can number, now rejoicing at the dazzling glory of those chosen souls that follow the Lamb whithersoever He goeth, now exulting in the magnificence of the martyrs with their crimson robes dyed in their own blood, now wondering at those stars of heaven, the teachers of God's people, of whom Holy Scripture declares that they shall shine with the brightness of the firmament, and as the stars for all eternity, because they have instructed many unto justice.

"Show us the Father," said the apostle St. Philip; "Lord, show us the Father, and it is enough." Show us the Father! Take away the veil that hides from us the face of God, and then, and not till then, the infinite void in our hearts will be filled! The world goes on its way, and the way of the world is evil. False christs and false prophets abound everywhere, and they are ever seeking to turn man away from his true end. They would try to persuade him that his happiness is in riches, in pleasures, in an equal distribution of power, in education, in himself, for there is a fashionable religion to-day which dethrones the all-perfect and eternal God, for a vague and pitiful deity called "humanity"! But it is all in vain; God gave us our nature and our nature cannot change; and those who listen to these false teachers only turn away in disappointment, and wander hither and thither crying out in the bitterness of an unsatisfied heart: *Quis ostendit nobis bona*—"Who will show us any good?" (Ps. 4:6). Only the Catholic faith can give an answer, and its answer is ever the same; God made man to know Him, to love Him, to serve Him in this world and to be happy with Him forever in the next. We see the same great truth solemnly affirmed by the Savior of the world Himself, when He had finished His work on earth, and for the last time gathered around Him His faithful friends and disciples to hear His words of farewell. "As the Father has loved me," He said to them, "I also have loved you. Abide in my love. If you keep my commandments you shall abide in my love, as I also have kept my Father's commandments and do abide in His love. These things I have spoken to you, that my joy may be in you and your joy may be filled" (John 15:9–11). And what was this joy of which He spoke and which He called "His joy," because so utterly beyond all reach of sorrow? It was the joy of His soul in the vision of the Godhead, the joy which He promised them and all His faithful servants when He said: "I will see you again, and your heart shall rejoice, and your joy no man shall take from you… Father, I will, that where I am, they also whom Thou hast given me may be with me, that they may see my glory which Thou hast given me, because Thou hast loved me before the creation of the world" (John 16:22; 17:24).

A few more words, and we are done. The very glory of heaven should fill us with fear and trembling. If the reward were less, it might seem more easy to deserve, more easy to obtain! But it is so infinitely great, and so easy to miss, and if it be missed? But it must not be missed; we must make up our minds to fight on until the end. The harder the struggle the more chance of success, if only we fight on bravely and perseveringly, for we serve a good Master, in whose eyes effort seems to count for victory. How can this earth have any real hold upon our hearts when heaven is placed before us? How can joys and pleasures, which at the best endure but for a day, make us risk a happiness which is eternal? As Catholics—nay, as reasonable beings—we should be ready to despise all, to risk all, to sell all in order to buy this pearl of great price, eternal life in the kingdom of God. Once we have made up our minds to this, life must be happy because it is the way to God, and death must be welcome because it comes to us as His messenger, changing into fruition the "hope that is laid up in our bosom," and dispelling forever the shadows of earth with words that are the revelation of heaven: "The Master is here, and calls thee" (John 11:28).

Part Two

The Working of Grace

I

Omnipotence and Freedom

If we may describe religion as the bond of union between God and man, it necessarily follows as a logical consequence that any form of religion which pretends to do away with mysteries, must, by that very fact, proclaim its own falseness and utter worthlessness. For God is infinite and man is finite, and therefore man can never comprehend God. In God there must be lofty heights which man can never climb, though the bright shining light of faith, touching their distant summits, makes us see that they are there. We call them, therefore, mysteries, and we feel that they are, and ever must be, an integral part of that one, true, and most holy religion revealed to man by his Creator. And amongst them all it would be hard to point out one more wonderful, more lofty, and more beautiful than that which hides from us the secret of God's dealings with His creatures. I say "hides from us," for when our faith has shown us all it can of this great mystery, it shows us so much that is terrifying and repellent, even when we feel it most attractive—so many strange, deep shadows, even when the light is brightest, or perhaps because of the very brightness of the light—that it hides as much as it reveals.

Faith in God implies belief in God's almighty power. We cannot say that we believe in God, unless we are willing at the same time to profess our faith in His supreme and absolute power over all the works of His hands. God made the world, and the world is ruled by Him, with a complete, universal, and unquestionable dominion. He looked out over the darkness of chaos, and spoke His word of power, "Let there be light," and the light was there. He spoke again, and the sun, and the moon, and the myriads of stars poured their floods of light though space, and swiftly sped along the mighty paths His hand had traced out for them. He looked down upon our little earth, and His creative word clothed it with life and beauty, and made it fit to be the dwelling place of man; and sun, and stars, and earth, and man must all submit to His almighty sway. His wisdom guides all, His power governs all, His influence permeates all—all, from the highest angel to the lowest form of matter; but not all in the same way. There is not a wider difference of nature between the mighty angel that bows down before the throne of God, and the senseless clod of earth, than there is between God's way of acting upon them. For the angel, like man, is free—and here is the mystery; for how is God almighty, if there be such a gift as freedom? How can the creature claim dominion over his own acts, if the Creator be the universal Master? This is the mystery we would examine and try to understand; this is the problem we would try to solve; and when we have most carefully considered the nature of the divine action on a free agent like our own soul, we may reverently direct our gaze to even higher ranges still, and contemplate that same mysterious and almighty power as it gently yet most surely carries on its marvelous work and guides man through the many winding paths of earthly life, towards that eternal life which is the glorious end and purpose of his creation.

Our first step is evident. Before we can attempt to examine difficulties, we must define our terms. What do we understand by freedom? What do we mean when we assert so boldly that man is free? Are we justified in the assertion, and is it really so very self-evident? In our doubts and difficulties, here as elsewhere, we cannot do better than appeal to St. Thomas, the Angel of the Schools: *laus et gloria Praedicatorum Ordinis*. And what does St. Thomas say about freedom? He tells us that it is the power of choosing, and that its proper and peculiar act is the act of choice[1]; and this definition is well worth our attention, for it lays bare the root of the difficulty. Everybody in this world desires happiness; but this desire is not an exercise of freedom. We cannot do otherwise. It is a necessity of our being, imposed upon us by our Maker. But we see the difference at once when it is a question of the means to be adopted. These we can and do choose for ourselves, and our choice is the deliberate act of our free will, so that freedom implies the act of choosing a particular object, without for a moment surrendering the power of abstaining from the choice. This faculty is man's most wonderful possession, most clearly distinguishing him from the lower orders of creation, and making him, in some way, the image of his Creator. That we really do possess this power of choice, this faculty of free will, is a dogma of the Catholic faith. Holy Scripture affirms it again and again. "In the beginning," says the Book of Ecclesiasticus, "God made man, and left him in the hand of his own counsel" (Eccles. 14:14). And so, in

1. *Proprium liberi arbitrii est electio* (*ST* I, q. 83, a. 3).

the same inspired pages, we see God condescending to plead with His own creatures; we hear Him imploring them to forsake their evil ways, and return to Him; we hear Him promising abundant rewards if they will hearken to His call, and threatening them with punishment if they refuse. But all this necessarily implies free will, the power of obedience and the power of disobedience, for otherwise the promise of reward would be a mockery, and the threat of punishment most cruel and unjust. So the Catholic Church has ever taught that man is free; and if we go a step further and examine this same question in the light of reason and experience, we shall be forced to confess that it is indeed most manifest and evident to all. For our understanding and our will are not two absolutely independent powers, working on their own lines and ignoring one another. On the contrary, they are linked together in the closest unity, and the laws which rule them are wonderfully alike. The understanding necessarily admits first principles, which are the basis of all reasoning; but when it is a question of the application of those principles, the arguments for and against are carefully weighed and considered, and so the final decision is made. The explanation of this is that in these matters the judgment is not determined beforehand, otherwise men in similar circumstances would always act in the same way. We have already shown that this is precisely similar to the action of the will, and so St. Thomas argues that man is necessarily free *because* he is a reasonable being. But surely the strongest argument of all is the intense conviction that exists in every mind. We feel that we are free. I take up my pen and write, and I know that I can cease writing when I choose. I lay down my pen, and no one can persuade me that I am not free to take it up again, if I choose. I may have reasons for what I do, but reasons are only the motives of my act. The principle or cause which gives it being is to be found in the will, and hence we are the authors of the act, and the responsibility of it lies upon our shoulders to bring us praise or blame, according as it is profitable or harmful to ourselves or those around us. Now, this is not the special pleading of a Catholic theologian. It is the common agreement of mankind. Why raise monuments to our great men? Why talk of great men at all? Why speak with respect and praise of a Shakespeare, a Newton, a Wellington, a Wilberforce, if their success was but the fruit of blind necessity? But we feel it is not so! We honor them because they strove so manfully to accomplish what they might have left undone—because they climbed to high success, when failure would have been accounted blameless. And as it is with praise, so it is with blame. The voice of public opinion crowns those whom it decrees to honor, and with equal right condemns and judges those who fail to reach the standard which it has created. For the failure is their own choice, and the condemnation is deserved. The standard of morality may vary, it may be more exacting sometimes than at others, but its variations have a limit; and that the limit may be kept in view, society proclaims its laws and the punishments which are to be the safeguards of their fulfillment. But all this implies free will, since right is born of justice, not of might, and justice is at once the offspring and the guardian of man's freedom. The very existence, then, of social life, its laws, its rewards, and its punishments, all proclaim emphatically that man is free. All are meant to prove, and prove most clearly, those words of Sacred Scripture: "God made man in the beginning and left him to be guided by his own counsel. He set fire and water before you; stretch forth your hand unto whichever you will. Before man is life and death; whichever he likes shall be given him, for the wisdom of the Lord is great" (Eccles. 14:14, 16–17).

We, hold, then as a certain truth, that we are free, that God has crowned His other gifts to man by the power of liberty, by which man is constituted master and responsible author of his own acts; and professing our firm adherence to this truth, we are now asked to believe that God is the Supreme Master of the universe, and that His almighty dominion extends to every single act of every one of His creatures. This must also be true, absolutely true; otherwise God would not be God at all. And because truth cannot oppose truth, we must find a way of reconciling what at first sight seems contradictory; and we must do this without trespassing in any way upon the infinite perfections of God, or those which He has bestowed upon His noblest handiwork. It is the fashion today to forget all this, and to exact man at the expense of God; and every common newspaper seems to make free will, or liberty, a sort of fetish, and to greet with loud and angry disapproval all who hesitate in their acceptance of it. We humbly listen to the teaching of our faith, which proclaims the liberty of man, subject to the absolute sovereignty of God.

How, then, does God govern His free creatures? First of all, of course, by His laws, for a law, as St. Thomas points out, is simply the manifestation of the will of the lawgiver, prescribing all that is to be done, and all that is to be avoided, in order that the general good may be secured. Manifestly, therefore, a good law is the best guardian of liberty, and God's laws are the outcome of goodness and wisdom that is infinite. We see them in the order and proportion of the things around us—the world in which we live; and, whether they admit it or not, it is only by a firm reliance on these laws that the astronomers or the men of science are able to continue their work, and every new discovery is another proof of their blind confidence. But just as there are laws to rule the elements and forces of the material world, so also are there laws for us. We have our special place in the universe, and our special laws—laws for the body, and laws for the soul. That divine Almighty Wisdom which ordains all things to their end, and which we call the Eternal Law of God, is reflected in the soul of man. The light of His countenance has been turned upon us, urging us to follow truth and goodness; for truth is the natural object of the mind and goodness is the natural object of the will. If we disobey, our reason and our will are conscious of this failure, and we hear within us the accusing voice of conscience telling us that we have sinned. But God has gone further. He has given us Ten Commandments. Clearly and definitely He has expressed His will, and He would have us hearken and obey. Yet we retain the power of free will. Though we cannot be independent, we can be disobedient, like the haughty ruler of Egypt; and then, if we persevere in our rebellion, there will one day come to us the awakening that the Red Sea brought to Pharaoh—for God remains the Master. "The Egyptians shall know," He said, "that I am the Lord" (Ex. 14:18).

But we have already said that the sovereignty of God is universal and absolute in every sense of the word; and we fail to see how this could possibly be the case, were it to find its limits in the mere communication of His will, and the final punishment of those who obstinately rebel against Him. The proclamation of a law is only moral guidance, and if God's action go no further, and we can say that all the movements of our own free will depend on us as on their first and only principle, then God's supremacy has found a limit, and He is not the First and all-pervading Cause. See what a world of thought is opened to us, as we survey these wondrous truths of faith, and note how cautiously we must proceed, for reason is ever hasty and impetuous, and here it must walk prudently, hand in hand with faith. A superficial mind might see no difficulty whatever, and base a premature conclusion on the old saying which reminds us that the author of a cause is the author of its effects as well (*quod est causa est causa causati*) and therefore since God made us as we are, and gave us our free will, He is the Cause of all we do, since He it was who gave us power to do it. So the locomotive runs along the metals, and safely drags the loaded wagons to the destination, or else perhaps it comes to ruin and destruction by swerving from the track, and falling over the embankment. Yet, after all, it was the driver's doing, since his hand turned the lever, and set the wheels in motion; and may we not then say that he was the cause? Comparisons, we know, are always more or less inadequate, but still this illustration, poor as it may be, suggests the answer to our difficulty, for God is not a cause like that. God knows all things, and cannot act in ignorance of the future. Accidents in His arrangements are impossible, and all results are clearly foreseen, and definitely arranged. And why? Because, as we have said, the infinite wisdom of our Creator has ordained all things for an end. In some mysterious way, the myriad beings of this mighty universe and all their myriad acts combine together to form one beautiful, harmonious whole. It follows, therefore, as a natural consequence, that God must know and foresee all: it follows that He must have known and foreseen all from all eternity; for He surely cannot vary His arrangement and eternal plan with every inconsistent variance of our unstable wills—He, the unchangeable God—"with whom there is no change, nor shadow of turning!" (James 1:17). But how can God foresee the acts of our free will, unless they are in some most special way dependent on Him, and on His causality? Even were you to suppose (as some do) that He could foresee them by some miracle of knowledge, which to me seems utterly impossible, the difficulty still remains, for how is He to bring to pass His own wise plans, and be in very deed and truth the first great Cause, if we are independent? God's universal knowledge and supreme dominion are at stake. You cannot save them, except by admitting the direct action of God's will upon our own. So, in the interests of God's absolute and universal sovereignty, as well as for the sake of His infinite knowledge, we hold that God must act on us and with us, in all the acts of our free will, even as He guides us by His commandments. Strongly, and yet most gently, as the Council of Trent points out, He moves all things to their end, penetrating them through and through with His almighty power, and yet in no way interfering with their powers as secondary causes. And since we and our free wills are secondary causes, He must act on us, and in us, and with us. "In Him, we live and move and have our being;" and in strict accordance with our nature, and perfecting the gift of liberty which He Himself bestowed, He works in us the power to will and to do—*operatur in nobis velle et perficere* (Philip. 2:13). So let us see how this is done, according to the various explanations of the schools, and how much of it is the teaching of our faith, and how much man's opinion.

There are some theologians[2] who teach that God's universal sovereignty, and the consequent dependence of the creature, are sufficiently explained by holding that God gives

2. The Molinist and Congruist Schools.

to all created causes a sort of general and indifferent help (*concursus*), "of such a nature that it does not incline the will to either side, but merely assists it, and bestows upon it the power to act as it chooses. The particular determination of the action is the outcome of the natural free activity of the created will,"[3] or, in other words, free will determines itself. Others, again, would have us see in the many circumstances of our life, the prearranged expression of God's will in our regard. They appeal also to that mighty moral force we call persuasion, a force most wonderful in every way, even in man's weak hands, but surely limitless when used by God. With all due deference to the learned men who have put forward these suggestions, we must confess they seem to us impossible and full of contradictions, and absolutely fatal to God's sovereignty. For, while admitting on the one hand that God's influence pervades all causes, so that He must be the immediate source of every operation, they still insist that there is something in the creation which is not from God, namely, the particular determination of the will, a real positive entity, therefore, of which the creature and not the Creator is the cause.

If we turn now to the teaching of St. Thomas, the great master and leader of the Thomist school of theologians, we shall see how it goes straight to the root of the difficulty. According to the Thomists, God's absolute dominion demands that He should be literally and truly the First Cause of all things—all beings and all modes of being, all powers and all operations. So that although a creature is endowed with the power of acting, and does really act—for otherwise its power would be superfluous, and the due order of cause and effect would be disturbed—it acts nevertheless in such a way that

3. Matteo Liberatore, S.J., *Theologia naturalis*, ch. 4.

its action also comes from God, First and Universal Cause. It must depend immediately upon God, and for this very simple reason. The actual exercise of the power of a created agent is a real mode of being, which previously did not exist: It is a new effect, a new being, and every sort of being essentially implies immediate dependence on the first cause, as the condition of its existence. For all created things depend immediately on God, their Maker and Preserver, and the divine Causality, as first and all-pervading, must necessarily act in all, so that there is no being, or possible mode of being, which can escape its influence.[4] In other words, just as no creature can live unless God gives it being, so neither can it act unless He moves it. The infinite causality of God necessarily postulates that all finite causality should entirely depend on Him as on the First Universal Cause of all being, and all mode of being. The Creator makes the creature. It cannot make itself. It follows, therefore, that no created agent can act unless moved by God, for by the causality of an agent we mean the actual exercise of its power. This divine motion is called by Thomists pre-motion, or pre-determination, physical or efficient pre-motion, for the act of the mover is prior to the motion of the object moved—not indeed in point of time, but in the order of reason and causation. But then, say the opponents of Thomists, what becomes of liberty, and how about sin? As regards liberty, St. Thomas makes the efficient motion of God the cause of our liberty. We are only free because God moves us. Liberty does not mean that the will is the master of its acts to the exclusion of the first cause, but God moves all in accordance with their natures, and as He makes the fire burn necessarily, so He makes man choose freely. That is to

4. Cf. Alberto Lepidi, O.P., *Ontologia*, lib. iii, sect. ii, ch. 3.

say, says St. Thomas, He causes the act, and its mode as well, for necessity or freedom are only the modes of the acts they specify. With regard to sin, we have only to remember that its malice is a pure negation, of which God cannot be the cause. Whatever there is of good in that material act which we call sin, belongs to God; the moral failure is to be attributed to our weak wills. These, then, are the various ways in which the saints and learned men have tried to throw light on this mystery. You are free to choose which you will, but your last appeal must be to faith. You must believe that God is Master, that we are not sufficient of ourselves to do anything, but that our sufficiency is from God (2 Cor. 3:5; Is. 26:12), and that He works all our works in us. And on the other hand you must believe that we are free to work out our salvation, to deserve eternal life or eternal death, since the responsibility of our acts is our own; you must believe that the will is not a mere machine, but a real active agent which positively cooperates with the divine motion, and never loses its perfect liberty of choice. These are the two ends of the chain, to which, as Bossuet says, we all must cling so firmly, even though the connecting links are hidden from our sight. It is only when our hold is firm and steady that we may venture to direct our steps to loftier heights, and contemplate God's supernatural action in the soul of man, the wonders of the world of grace. Bright as may have been the light we have already gazed upon, it is far brighter here; dark as may have been the shadows cast around us, they are darker here. It is a supernatural world, a world of saints and angels, and earnest, patient, toiling men and women, and one and all bear witness to the familiar words of the Apostle: "By the grace of God, I am what I am, and His grace in me has not been void."

II

The Necessity of Grace

Everybody is familiar with the Parable of the Good Samaritan. It is one of those wonderful pictures drawn by the hand of our Blessed Lord Himself, and meant to convey a special lesson, not merely to those who first received it, but to every soul in every age. In it our Lord most graphically describes the miserable state of our race in consequence of the sin of our first parents, and at the same time points out to us the gracious work which He, our Savior, had come into this world to accomplish. He tells us of a traveler who fell into the hands of robbers, and, after being grievously wounded, was left to perish by the roadside, and was there found by a charitable Samaritan who happened to be passing by. That poor traveler is the type of our race, forsaking Jerusalem, the city of peace, and all the joys of innocence, for Jericho, the city of confusion, and so falling into the hands of Satan, by whom it was deprived of its glorious gifts, sorely wounded in its natural faculties, and left in misery, and wretchedness, subject to death. For God in His goodness had created man in a state altogether above his nature. He might have been content to bestow upon him the perfection of all natural gifts, and nothing further; but that was not His will. His design was grander, nobler, in every way. He made man in His own image and likeness, by giving him a spiritual and immortal soul, and He destined that soul to a special union with Himself, enabling it to see Him face to face, and dwell with Him forever. But as this destiny was altogether supernatural, it was necessary that God should bestow upon men some supernatural principle as a means to this supernatural end. His nature had to be changed and elevated, and God achieved this by creating Him in the state of grace, or what we usually call the state of original justice. It would take long to describe the happiness of that state—a life of peace, and tranquil joy, and frequent converse with God and the angels—a life which possessed the fullness of all knowledge—the perfection of all virtues—the control of all the passions—a life independent of sickness, suffering, and death—and all this because of that first and special gift of sanctifying grace![1] And then came the fall! "By one man," says St. Paul, "sin came into this world, and by sin, death, and so death passed upon all men, because all have sinned" (Rom. 5:12). All have sinned! "This gift of original justice," says St. Thomas, "was given to our parents under certain conditions, to be passed on to their posterity; and when, because of their sin, they lost it, their posterity lost it also. And by this, God is not unjustly punishing the children for the sin of their parents; He is only taking away a gift to which they have no right whatever, but which He would have given them through their parents had they not willfully lost the power of transmitting it."[2] And the Angel-

1. *ST* I, q. 94, etc.
2. Thomas Aquinas, *Compendium of Theology*, II, ch. 195.

ic Doctor gives the example of a title or an estate given to a family on certain fixed conditions, and then lost by the treason or violation of these conditions on the part of one of their members. So we are born into this world, stripped of sanctifying grace and the friendship of God, and all those wonderful gifts which were the fruits of it. And not only are those gifts lost to us, but our very nature is weakened and spoiled in many ways. Our minds are darkened, our wills are weakened, our passions are strengthened and in unceasing rebellion. We may have seen or heard of those fierce storms that come and go so swiftly, yet mark their passage on the face of nature by ruin and destruction that seem irreparable. In the morning the sun rises on a smiling landscape, a busy town, with many stately buildings framed in fields and vineyards and lofty forest trees; and ere he sinks in the western sky on that same evening, an awful change has taken place. What was the busy town is now a heap of stones, though one or two firm buildings may remain to mark the ruined streets. The gardens and the vineyards are wasted and uprooted, and the few trees that have withstood the fury of the storm are stripped of their branches and their leaves. A supernatural storm has swept across that human nature upon which God looked with love, and blessed because it was so good, and we have seen how awful was its work of devastation. Yet all the good was not destroyed. The light which shone within man's mind to show him good from evil, still was there; the natural inclination of the will towards good was also there, though somewhat bent towards earth and earthly things by the strength of passions in revolt; and therefore we may say his natural powers remained substantially the same as they would have been had God never crowned him with the gift of grace, but hampered by the numerous obstacles which now beset his path. For his will, as we have just admitted, was bent away from God, its last end in the order of grace as well as nature; in casting off God's friendship he had likewise cast away God's gracious help and guardianship, and, finally, he had placed himself within the power of Satan, the robber and murderer of souls. Most wretched, therefore, was his plight. Robbed and wounded grievously, and dying by the roadside, what could he do? And then to him, in that dark hour of utter misery and despair, there came the Good Samaritan, bending over him with tenderest pity, cleansing and healing his wounds, and bearing him to a place of safety. So, when our first father heard God's judgment on his sin, and realized his loss, the light of hope, which we may well believe had almost died away within his soul, was once more fanned into a flame by the loving promise of a Savior who was to be the Good Samaritan of our race, and heal its wounds, and carry out God's glorious plans, with a grander and more perfect beauty. Adam had received the headship of mankind, and from him we have all received our human nature; another Adam was to come, whose headship was to be in every sense more noble, for "grace and truth" were to come back to us by Him, and "of His fullness we have all received"; and our faith tells us that this second Adam was no other than Almighty God Himself, Jesus Christ our Savior! Most wonderful was His work. We call it *salvation*: "He shall save His people from their sins" (Matt. 1:21); *redemption*: "He has wrought the redemption of His people" (Luke 1:68); *reconciliation*: "God was in Christ, reconciling the world with Himself" (2 Cor. 5:19). And so St. Paul writing to the Colossians sums it all up and urges us to be grateful, "giving thanks unto the Father, who has made us worthy to be partakers of the inheritance of the saints in light, who has delivered us from the power of darkness, and has translated us into the kingdom of the Son of His love" (Col. 1:12). Indeed so great are the benefits of this great work of our Savior that the Church seems almost to bless God for having permitted the Fall. "O truly needful sin of Adam, which was blotted out by the death of Christ! O happy fault which deserved to possess such a Redeemer."[3] For, in the state of innocence, man saw and worshipped the magnificent liberality of his Maker; now he adores His boundless mercy. In the state of innocence, God's help was less abundant, because less needed; now it comes as flights of angels, though their faces may be hidden with the veils of suffering and temptation. In the state of innocence, man walked along a flowery road towards eternal happiness, sheltered all the while beneath the shadow of God's wings; now he struggles up a steep and thorny path, but God is nearer, and clasps him firmly by the hand.

Let us therefore now go into this more closely, and see how necessary for us in our fallen state is this most gracious help and strong assistance from on high, which we call grace. Taking the word, in its very widest sense, we might truly say that every gift bestowed on us by God was a grace or favor; but when we speak of the *necessity* of grace, we are considering it precisely as a *help*, and so we understand by it any favor gratuitously bestowed on us by God to enable us to carry out, easily and successfully, the end of our creation. This definition is a true one, though somewhat wide and general, and it would be easy to content ourselves with it, and, making it our starting point, go on to show our absolute dependence on these heavenly favors. But, even at the risk of being wearisome, we must try to be a little more precise, and

3. Office for Holy Saturday.

at the same time do our best to make our meaning clear. It is easy to be general, and tiring to the mind to be precise, and our natural tendency is to choose the easy path, and shirk a difficulty when we can lawfully do so. Now the ideas of most of us about "nature" and "grace" are very general, very vague, and often very incorrect; and so a word or two seems necessary to prevent misunderstanding. What is of nature, we are apt to think, is all our own—is natural—and what is not of nature is unnatural, coming to us from without; and when the Catechism tells us that grace is a supernatural gift of God, we make a sort of antithesis between grace and nature, and look upon them and their operations as separate and independent, though more or less united now and then in some accidental way. So, in the days of chivalry, the soldier clothed himself from head to foot in burnished armor, and with his sword and lance and shield went forth to battle, and his victory depended on the quality of his armor and the temper of his weapons, as much as on the strength of his right arm. Now it would never do to speak or judge of grace and nature as in any way resembling the soldier and his armor. Our last chapter was meant to save us from that error, for if we listen to the teaching of St. Thomas, we must see in grace a vital principle in the soul, by which it really acts, so that every effect of grace is really and truly wholly from man, at the same time that it is really and truly wholly from God. With this important truth before our minds, we may reverently and briefly analyze the idea of a supernatural aid from God, bestowed upon us, as we said, gratuitously, and moving us towards that supernatural good which is the end of our creation. How, then, can God do this? He can directly pour upon our souls His sanctifying grace and all those different virtues which complete its beauty; or, as the first cause in the order of grace, He may impress upon us a supernatural influence, directly moving us to supernatural acts and deeds of virtue, or He may so arrange the accidents of life and our surroundings that they become positive helps to us in our work. The first and last ways surely need no explanation, but the second one claims our attention, as it is so philosophical and so profoundly true. How, then, does God move us to supernatural acts? First of all, by showing us, in all its beauty and attraction, the good work He would have us do, and also, in some cases, by pouring on the mind a flood of light enabling it to see and value all the beauty of that act. Then, over and above this moral influence, mighty as it is, God, as the First efficient Cause, can act directly on the will without in any way impairing His great gift of freedom. In our last chapter we have seen how He does this, applying the power which He has created by that motion which we Thomists call efficient motion, and without which no power, however perfect, can ever act at all. But sometimes God does more than this. Over and above this application of the existing power, He transiently bestows upon the soul another and a higher power, as, for instance, when He gently touches and moves towards the thoughts of higher things, some poor neglected soul, in which, because of sin and ignorance, there seems no vestige of the supernatural world.

After this brief but most important explanation, it is easy enough to see and understand the general teaching of the Church, so profoundly impressed upon the truly humble and religious heart, and so eagerly welcomed by it, that in the work of our salvation, all depends upon the help of God's grace; and that, although we really do the works which please Him and merit His reward, yet is it ever God Himself who makes us work with Him and use our freedom in the way that He desires. If we venture to think otherwise, if we dare to claim for our free will any good whatever, independently of God, we fall into that horrible heresy of Pelagius—an ancient heresy, perhaps, and yet most prevalent today, when it is the fashion to claim as a sign of the times all that can flatter self-confidence and self-reliance. And although it is quite true that the words of Holy Scripture and the Fathers, which might be quoted as a proof of what we hold, refer primarily to supernatural works, yet they most certainly do not exclude good works of a merely natural order. Our Catholic instinct is at once in arms against any such exclusion. Our faith and reason teach us the entire dependence of all created good on Him who is the Highest Good, and the only cause of good in others. They show us likewise that God's absolute independence necessarily forbids that He should be a debtor to the work of His hands, and hence His gifts must be gratuitous, even those which He seems bound to give, since He it is who gives the merit, and so creates the obligation (Cf. Romans 11:35). Whatever good there is or may be in the creature, of whatever order, or whatever degree, all comes to it from its Creator. Creatures are but the recipients of His goodness, and from His ever-flowing and abundant streams they have filled the tiny vessels He has made for them and placed at their disposal. "What do you have," says St. Paul, "that you have not received?" (1 Cor. 4:7). And hence it is that there are many things which, at first sight perhaps, may not appear to be a help from God, yet when more closely viewed by faith and reason, are seen most manifestly to be the tokens of His watchful love.

It will not do, therefore, to content ourselves with saying that God has given us the power of doing good and that we may do the rest; it will not do to qualify God's work in any way: clearly and distinctly St. Thomas teaches that all the good in every action is to be referred to God for not only is He the author of the life which acts, and the power by which it acts, but, as we have already seen, it is He who moves those powers in each and every one of their appropriate acts, and therefore, as the First Cause and Highest Good, He claims whatever being and whatever good there is in any of His creatures.

Granting all this, then, as a necessary preliminary, we turn to that first and noblest power bestowed by God on man—his understanding. Its object is the truth, and truth wherever it may be found; and no sooner are the faculties sufficiently developed, and the use of reason properly attained, than man begins to lean upon his understanding and listen to its dictates. And what can it show him? How far can it take him? It can show him those self-evident truths which we call first principles, and many conclusions which follow from them, and it can do this without any special help from God, although, of course, it always depends on that divine motion or impulsion of which we have already spoken. But it cannot go very far. Original sin has not destroyed man's nature, but it has wounded it in many ways, and the first and greatest wound inflicted on it is the wound of ignorance, which weakens the reasoning powers and hampers them on every side. Man no longer possesses that pure and ardent love of knowledge which was the outcome of his perfect nature, and the way of knowledge is to him a thorny path, where progress means hard work and constant application. His health and strength moreover are easily exhausted, his imagination is easily distracted, the cares of life are an incessant, ever present worry, and the very teachers whom he chooses as his guides are as hampered as himself. We might go on to show how even those great truths which form the basis of all moral order become obscured, and well-nigh utterly forgotten, when man is left to guide himself; but we have said enough to prove most clearly the need man has of God's assistance in the ordinary working of his intellectual life. When we mount higher, and consider those great truths revealed to us by God, our weakness is more manifest. It cannot be denied, of course, that when these truths are put before a man, his reason may assent to them from motives which are purely natural, as, for instance, owing to the influence of his early education, the love he has for those who taught him, or perhaps because his worldly career would suffer by an overt act of disbelief. For an assent like this, no special aid is necessary; but if we speak of an assent which rests on the reverence due to God, or the manifest excellence of these truths, then though there be in such an act no vestige even of the supernatural, we hold he cannot give it unless supported by God's grace. "The natural man," says St. Paul, "receives not the things of the Spirit of God, for they are foolishness to him; neither can he know them, because they are spiritually discerned" (1 Cor. 2:14).

The second great power of the soul is the will, by which man is carried forward to the good which he desires. We need not ask ourselves if the will can perform a *supernatural* work independently of God's assistance. The very word "supernatural" tells us that such a work is beyond the power of man; but we are speaking here exclusively of good actions in the natural order, and many and various are the opinions which at one time or another have been brought forward. Some have gone so far as to assert that all actions which are purely natural and unblessed by sanctifying grace are mortal sins, while others have maintained that faith at all events is a *sine qua non* in every good work. The Church has ever maintained the contrary; she has clearly defined in the great Council of Trent[4] that the state of grace is not necessary for the performance of a natural good work, and by the unanimous voice of her theologians she teaches that not even faith is necessary. We hold, then, that without any special help whatsoever, beyond the ordinary general guidance of divine Providence, man is able to perform good actions in the natural order. It follows from what we have already said of man's intelligence. His nature is not wholly spoiled, and so his will retains its natural inclination towards good, and only needs the ordinary guidance of its Maker to carry out the good work it desires. But when we turn our eyes towards Him who in the natural order is the First great Good, even the Creator Himself, and ask ourselves if by its own unaided power the will of man is able to cleave to Him, and love Him first and best and above all things, then must we answer in the negative. Man can and does elicit of himself (always supposing the natural guiding influence of God) a weak, imperfect sort of love for that great Being whom his reason has revealed to him; but to prefer Him to all else, to realize that He is our last end, and that all we do must be the loving tribute of our service—all this supposes the healing grace and kind assistance of our Maker. But if this be the case, if we depend on God so utterly for help to keep this first great law, what must be our dependence when brought face to face with all the Ten Commandments? Pelagius foolishly and wickedly asserted that of his own strength man could keep them all, while in the sixteenth century some of the "Reformers" held that, even with God's grace, obedience was impossible. Against all these we

4. Council of Trent, Session VI, ch. 7

must believe that man most certainly depends on God's assistance to enable him to keep God's law in all things, and that, moreover, help is never wanting in each particular case. And when we think how these same laws of God, which in themselves may not seem very hard or burdensome, are often made so by our weakness and the strange power of temptation, we see again, and still more clearly, our pressing need of help. For though the natural love of honesty and decency may sometimes keep a man from yielding to his foes, yet when we contemplate the number of these foes and their variety, their dreadful subtlety and skill, and our weakness; when we see how the good that we will, we do not, and the evil that we would not, we do, we begin to understand St. Paul's cry of anguish: "Wretched man that I am, who shall deliver me from the body of this death?" (Rom. 7:19, 24). And the Apostle himself gives the answer: "The grace of God, by Jesus Christ our Lord." It is grace which shows us God's law, grace which keeps us faithful to it, grace which helps us when the yoke seems galling, grace which lifts us up when we have fallen; and, above all, it is grace which strengthens us to go on fighting to the end, and sends the angel of death to us in the glad moment of victory.

What a wonderful light is cast upon our life by the thought of all this, and the consequent realization of our utter dependence on God our Father. He has made us for Himself, to be the sharers of His eternal glory; and for this high end, our natural gifts considered in themselves are simply useless, so He gives us grace, and all is easy. Why, then, let the thought of our weakness distress us? The King of Syria sent his horses and chariots and a host of armed men to compass the city in which God's prophet dwelt; and the sight of so many foes struck terror into the heart of the prophet's servant, so that he cried out: "Alas, my master, what shall we do?" And the prophet answered, "Fear not, for there are more with us than with them." And the Lord opened the eyes of the servant, and he saw, and lo, the mountain was covered with horses and chariots of fire, gathered together to protect them. So man walks along the pathway of life, weak and frail, and often stumbling in the darkness, and ever surrounded by snares and manifold temptations; but every step brings fresh and plenteous succor from the unseen world of grace, and as he perseveres and bravely struggles on, the darkness fades away before the increasing light, until at last he sees the dawn of the eternal day: "The path of the just, as the shining light, goes forward and increases unto the perfect day" (Prov. 4:18).

III

The Nature of Grace

The mere fact of our existence in this world is very wonderful, and suggestive of many thoughts. The varied beauty and attractions of nature, and the power of its multitudinous laws, the extent of our own mental gifts, and the greatness of our capabilities, the possible consequences of combined social effort—these, and many other similar thoughts, must pass before our minds, whenever we seriously reflect on those words of Sacred Scripture: "In the beginning, God created the heavens and the earth." Surely no intellectual mind can dwell on all this without wonder and amazement. Yet how much greater must be our wonder, how much deeper our amazement, when we remember that all these natural beauties of the universe, all our powers, and all our labors, here below, are meant as stepping stones to something higher and nobler in every way—the real ultimate end for which all was made. For "God made man in His own image and likeness," and the one end to which all else is absolutely subordinate is the completed perfection of that image and likeness, a perfection which can only be attained in the next life, when the soul sees its Maker face to face. Our end, then, is the vision of God, the sight of God, the knowledge of God as He is Himself, an end so wonderful, so supernatural in every way, that God could not make a creature with a natural right to such a blessedness, and so we see why He has given us grace; for grace is the power which enables us to attain this supernatural end. It is, therefore, a gift, a marvelous gift, a gratuitous gift, a created gift—a manifestation of divine power and goodness equivalent to a new creation. It bestows upon man a supernatural life with supernatural powers, a supernatural beauty beyond earthly imagination, a supernatural dignity beyond all deserts. We may have many natural gifts, or but a few; they may be of the highest order, or the lowest; as regards this supernatural end, they are, looked at in themselves, equally useless; but grace comes and takes possession of them, and penetrates them, and rules them, and makes them the ready instruments of its most perfect work. How often in our childhood's days have we not read with breathless interest some absorbing fairy tale, in which the hero of the story found himself opposed in every way by strange, mysterious, unseen foes, who harassed him at every step; and all the while he was helped on by powers equally strong and strange and wonderful—unseen spirits weaving potent spells and bringing triumph just when all seemed lost. But no tale of fairyland, however wonderful, could ever hope to equal the wonders of the supernatural world of grace, the home of God's dear children, the world in which they live and move, and have their being, surrounded by all sorts of heavenly powers and agencies. Today we want to enter this supernatural world, and study the nature of this mighty gift of God. For grace is, as we have said, a gift—a gift in every way above our nature, and yet so absolutely necessary to it, that, without it, human nature at its best seems a poor failure, a wonderful construction of divine power, spoiled and broken, and well-nigh altogether useless.

When, in the sixteenth century, the wickedness of men had provoked God's anger and so made possible that triumph of the powers of darkness so foolishly miscalled the "Reformation," one of the very first dogmas of the Catholic faith attacked by the miserable agents of Satan was this same dogma of grace. For the Catholic faith is not a heap of loose and disconnected stones, from which the passer-by may choose according to his own disordered fancy; it is a stately building put together by the all-wise God Himself, and put together in such a way that each stone has its fixed and proper place. To remove one, therefore, or to change the place of one, is to disarrange the whole, and we have but to glance through some of the so-called tenets of these first Reformers, to see at once how one denial led them to another, and plunged them into endless contradictions. The Catholic teaching with regard to grace was a barrier, an impassable barrier, to the acceptance of their theories about faith and good works, and so the Catholic teaching had to be denied. In place of it they ventured to assert that when a soul received from God the gift of grace, it did not thereby undergo a change. It was not cleansed, or healed, or purified, but it was clothed as with a garment, in the saving merits of Christ, and so although the hideous foulness of the work of sin might go on festering in that soul until the end of life, God saw it not; and, therefore, judged it not. The rebel wore the uniform of the King, and for its sake the obstinate rebellion and persistent treachery was overlooked. In their eyes, therefore, grace was nothing more than crediting the sinner, or "imputing" to the sinner, as it was called, the justice of his Savior, and the evidence of grace was to be found in a most firm conviction in the sinner's mind that this was the case, and that, in consequence, salvation was secure, no matter how he lived.

The Catholic doctrine, on the other hand, clearly defined and promulgated in the Eleventh Canon of the Sixth Session of the Council of Trent, utterly rejects this most preposterous theory, and declares sanctifying grace to be a real gift of God, changing, renewing, and regenerating the soul, and giving it a new life of such a nature as to make it in a special way the friend and child of God. Countless are the beautiful expressions in Sacred Scripture in which this doctrine is laid down. It is a "new spirit" and a "new heart" (Ez. 36:26; Rom. 5:5), which God promises to give to His repentant children, and the change is brought about in no other way than by the gift of the Holy Spirit, diffusing, or pouring into our hearts, the love and grace of God.

For what do we mean by grace? Surely nothing less than that divine, most gracious operation by which man's soul is made pleasing and acceptable in God's sight, or in other words, the outpouring of divine love upon the soul of man. Now, we cannot say that this is merely superficial or external. Love is that longing in the will for goodness, since goodness is the natural object of the will. Whoever loves, therefore, is drawn by goodness, real or apparent; and the lowest sinner that the world has ever seen indulges in his wickedness and loves it, because his darkened reason foolishly suggests that it is good. And this is true of all love—human or divine—but with this tremendous difference, that whereas all earthly love is attracted by the goodness which exists, or which it fondly imagines to exist, entirely independent of it, divine love is the source and fountain of all goodness, and must therefore necessarily cause it in the objects of its choice. Now see what this implies. The Creator can never look with favor on His creature, God's love can never rest on man, without producing in him at that moment the particular goodness which He loves, the special attraction which is pleasing in His sight. And the greater the love, the higher the perfection it produces. Man's health and strength, and all the varied powers of soul and body, are the effects of God's love in the natural order; and in that higher order, which is supernatural, God's love must cause a supernatural goodness which we call grace. And that is why, as Catholics, we maintain that grace is really and truly an internal gift of God poured into the soul, sanctifying it, and making it truly beautiful in His eyes. St. Thomas sums up very briefly all we have been saying. It is grace, he says, which makes us pleasing in God's sight. And this cannot be a mere external acceptance on the part of God, for it implies that we are the objects of God's infinite love. Therefore grace must be an altogether intrinsic effect, produced in the soul of man by its Creator. So when we think of sin and its deformity, and the hatred which Almighty God must have for it, we feel that when love takes the place of hatred, and that deformity has disappeared, it is not merely hidden from the sight of Him whose holiness it outraged, but it has absolutely ceased to be. And we must not forget, moreover, that this glorious gift of grace of which we are speaking is not a mere transient influence from on high, a passing blessing from the hand of Him from whom is every good and every perfect gift; it is, on the contrary, a permanent habit of the soul, the highest, the best, the most perfect of all, where all are so high, so good, and so perfect.

Now let us go a step further in order to still further illustrate our idea of grace. There are some Catholic theologians who maintain that grace is really the same as "charity," or the love of God. It is in reality, they say, one and the same gift of God, but it has different names according to the point of view from which you see it. It is charity, they say, if you would look upon it as our tribute to Almighty God; but if you view it rather as God's gift to us, then is it called grace. When it moves us to the love of God and to a greater diligence in His service, it is called charity; but when it draws God's love down upon us, then is it called grace. There are many theologians who have been upholders of this theory; but it is not the teaching of St. Thomas. The Angelic Doctor most distinctly insists on a real difference between them, as real as that which distinguishes human nature from its powers, since grace is placed by God within the very essence of the soul, while love may truly be called its manifestation in the great faculty of free will. And this opinion of St. Thomas seems based on Holy Scripture, for though the inspired writers frequently apply the name of grace to all the gifts of God, yet over and over again they use it in a more special and peculiar way to signify a gift distinct from all others; a gift which in itself unites us to Almighty God, and is the overflowing fountain of all other gifts, love itself included. So we have St. Paul's most beautiful and expressive words pointing out to us how the Holy Spirit Himself is given to us, and His love poured upon our hearts, in order to enkindle in them that return of love which He so ardently desires. And the beloved disciple, appealing to our sense of gratitude, urges us to give our love to God, since He has first loved us. But the love of God for us, as we have seen, is the gift of grace, and the return of love from our poor hearts is charity, and they are certainly distinct one from the other. Love glorifies the will of man, but grace itself is the high dowry of the soul itself, the riches and treasures of the very essence of his spiritual being. And with this we come to the very heart of the subject—where human words seem to fail us, so unspeakable is the grandeur of the teaching of our faith. So we turn to Holy Scripture for our final definition of God's grace, and it is St. Peter himself, the inspired Apostle, and First Vicar of our Savior, who tells us what it is and what we must believe. "Jesus Christ," says St. Peter, "has given us great and precious promises, that by these you might be made partakers of the divine Nature" (2 Pet. 1:4). Of ourselves we should never have dared to use such words. In the sacred pages may be found many expressions which seem strange in their sublimity, but these words of St. Peter have a wonder, and a grandeur, and a sublimity all their own. The just are said to be "born of God" (1 John 3:1; Ps. 82:6). He is called our "Father," and we are the sons of the Most High, the "brethren" of Christ; but magnificent as these titles are, they seem to fade into insignificance before the words of the Prince of the Apostles, "partakers of the divine Nature." What can they mean? Listen to St. Thomas, never so truly the Angelic Doctor as when treating of these high, unearthly subjects. "The gift of grace," he says, "is nothing less than a participation of the divine Nature, inasmuch as by it God makes us God-like, bestowing upon us, as it were, a share of the divine Nature."[1] But, you will say, how can this be? What does it mean? Grace cannot be a real participation of the divine Nature, with its infinite, incommunicable attributes! Such a doctrine seems impossible, and the words of St. Peter, and all those other wonderful expressions in Sacred Scripture to which we alluded just now, ought surely to be taken as figures of speech, and not as definitions of a literal truth. And yet, says St. Thomas, that is just what they are—

1. *ST* I-II, q. 112, a. 1.

definitions inspired by Almighty God—definitions of a literal truth. It is quite true, of course, that the Godhead, or the divine Nature, cannot be communicated to any creature outside itself, in such a way as to become the essence or nature of that creature. (We put aside altogether, as quite outside our subject, the adorable mystery of the Incarnation.) The divine Nature belongs solely to the three divine Persons, but it can be communicated by a gift, which, though distinct from it in every way, yet bestows upon the recipient such a likeness and resemblance as to deserve being called a participation of the divine Nature, and carries with it rights and privileges which seem to belong to God alone. This is beautifully expressed by the Bishop of Newport. "No created nature," says his lordship, "can by its natural resources ever look on the Face of God. To be able to see God is a prerogative of God alone. God could not create a nature which should include amongst the faculties or powers due to it, such a power as we speak of. Yet God in His infinite love has given to angels and men the power to see the bliss of His face inverted. This gift, beyond and exceeding all natural endowments, is supernatural, and its essence lies in this—that it lifts the soul of the creature so high, or, we may say, intensifies its powers so indescribably, that it can look on God; and therefore St. Peter, in a phrase that we thank and bless him for, affirms that it makes us partakers of the very nature of God."[2]

What a revelation of God's love in all this, and what a revelation of man's dignity! The perfection of that dignity can only be secured after death; but even in this life, such is God's generous love, man is crowned with the glory and honor of the divine adoption, and endowed with the blessedness of

2. Hedley, *Retreat*, p. 60–61.

heaven. When God made man from the dust of the earth, He breathed into him the breath of life, and man became a living soul. When He bestows upon him the gift of grace, He breathes into him the breath of everlasting life. "The grace of God is everlasting life," and man enters upon a life that can know no end as long as the breath of grace animates his soul. What a wonderful thought! Surely all other ideas of life are vain and unreal, and unworthy of our attention! God has given us all so many gifts, our body and soul, our life, our health and strength, our talents, our prospects, our friends—all come to us from Him. And yet these gifts, great as they are, numerous as they are, and full as they are of well-nigh countless possibilities, have no real usefulness save when made subordinate to grace. For God did not make us merely to pass our lives in pleasant occupation; He did not make us only to succeed in our various careers, and so win for ourselves the reward of success, a comfortable living, or an honored name—He did not make us merely to live; but He made us to live forever; He made us—how familiar and how old-fashioned are the words, and yet how little realized by most of us—He made us to know Him, to love Him, and to serve Him in this world, and to be happy with Him forever in the next. And just as grace helps us in our knowledge, love, and service of Him, just as it bestows upon us everlasting happiness in the next world, so will it give us real happiness in this. Indeed, all other happiness is but a dream compared with the joy and gladness that are born of this wonderful communion of the soul with God, this intimate service of the great Master "who gives joy to our youth." What would it avail us to win and enjoy all other happiness, if we lose this? "What does it profit a man, if he gain the whole world, and lose his own soul?" "Whosoever is wise shall give heed to these things, and they shall consider the mercies of the Lord" (Ps. 107). We are, therefore, wise or foolish, good or bad, according as we do our best to realize these things, or treat them with indifference. The one work of life is the right appreciation of grace—a most serious thought, full of fears for the careless, full of encouragement for those who are in earnest.

IV

The Action of Grace

The concluding thought of our last chapter was the conviction that the great work of life was the right use of grace. From this it follows very naturally that the great want of life will be a more perfect knowledge of grace and its working in our soul. The best of us are more or less touched with worldliness, and worldliness tends to make us ignore grace altogether. By worldliness we mean that unseen power which is capable of supplying the soul, the heart of man, with interesting things that have no reference to God. Its natural effect is to make us careless about our eternal interests—our real interests. It inclines us to rely absolutely on ourselves, and makes us instinctively side against God; and its most efficient antidote is the knowledge of our grace. We have defined grace as that wonderful and gratuitous favor on the part of God which raises the soul of man to a state of supernatural perfection, or, to speak more precisely, it is a gratuitous supernatural gift of God, bestowed upon us in order to forward the work of our salvation. We call it "supernatural" to distinguish it from those many natural gifts and powers and talents, so liberally bestowed upon us by our Maker, although by no means wishing to exclude that gracious interference of divine Providence in the many commonplace circumstances of our daily lives. For the very first thought that comes to our minds, when we begin to study the action of grace upon our soul, is that some graces seem to be altogether external in their mode of operation, whereas others act directly upon the innermost sanctuary of the heart. What we often call the accidental circumstances of our life—our birth in a Christian country, with religious surroundings—our education, our knowledge of God's law, the reading of a good book or the hearing of a sermon, the chance of doing some good work, or obstacles in the way of sin and temptation—all these are in reality so many tokens of the watchful care and loving protection of our heavenly Father, who has declared that not one hair of our head can fall to the ground without His knowledge. St. Augustine points this out in one of his sermons. "Thou didst not fall into sin, because the tempter never came; he never came because I forbade it; the time and place were unfavorable for sin: it was I who so arranged it. Recognize, then, the work of my grace."[1]

Those graces which, on the other hand, seem to act directly on the soul, may be divided into two classes according as they are destined primarily for the salvation of our own soul or the souls of others. We say primarily destined, for we see at once that the sanctification of one's own soul is in itself, and must be, a silent sermon to all around us, and we cannot hope to draw other souls nearer to God unless at the same time we try to draw nearer ourselves. In that part of his first epistle to the Corinthians which is read on the tenth Sunday

1. Lib. i, Hom. 23.

after Pentecost, St. Paul enumerates these graces which are mainly given for the help of others, and which theologians call *gratis datae*. We must remember, of course, that all graces are *gratis datae*, but the term has come to be applied to these, just as we call the brute creation "animals," though, strictly speaking, it applies to men as well. "The manifestation of the Spirit," says St. Paul, "is given to every man unto profit. To one indeed by the Spirit is given the *word of wisdom*, and to another the *word of knowledge*, according to the same Spirit; to another, *faith* in the same Spirit; to another the *grace of healing* in one Spirit, to another the *working of miracles*, to another *prophecy*, to another the *discerning of spirits*, to another, diverse *kinds of tongues*, to another *interpretation of speeches*" (1 Cor. 12:7:10). St. Thomas[2] most beautifully comments on these words of St. Paul, justifying the enumeration given by the Apostle; and even at the risk of being tedious, we may very briefly refer to the Angelic Doctor. There are three things, he says, necessary for the work of putting the faith before others, and convincing them of its truth. There must be the fullness of knowledge in the teacher, the ability to prove and confirm what he says, and the power of placing it intelligibly before his hearers. For the first, says St. Thomas, the teacher must be absolutely certain about the principles of religion, and so he receives what St. Paul calls the grace of faith; he must draw the right conclusions from these principles, and he does this by the word of wisdom; he must also be able to illustrate his teaching by examples from nature and her laws, and the word of knowledge helps him to do this. The second qualification implies supernatural powers, because articles of faith cannot be proved by arguments

2. *ST* I-II, q. 3, a. 4.

of reason, hence he receives the grace of healing, or the still higher grace of miracles in general, or the power of prophecy and discernment of spirits. And the third requirement necessitates a knowledge of the language of those to whom he is speaking, or the gift of tongues, and also the clear understanding of divine revelation, the interpretation of speeches.

It goes without saying that these graces are altogether of an inferior order to those which are given for the sanctification of our own soul, since of themselves they do not unite as to Almighty God. And so in the very next chapter of the same epistle, St. Paul goes on to speak of the more excellent way, which, though outwardly less glorious, brings the soul into immediate relationship with its Maker. And here again we have various subdivisions, according to the particular work that grace may seem to do. Sometimes, as we have already seen, it is an actual impulse from above, moving the understanding and the heart to carry out the will of God; and sometimes, on the contrary, it must be looked at rather as a permanent gift, or supernatural habit, conferred by God upon the soul to fit it for the carrying out of the divine plan. Sometimes we may consider it as beginning the good work in the soul, and at another time strengthening the heart to persevere in toil, and finish the good work so gloriously begun. Sometimes it wakes us from the heavy sleep of sin, and opens our eyes to the necessity of repentance; sometimes, like a guardian spirit, it hovers over us to spur us onward, and save us from the fate of those who yield to weariness, and slumber by the roadside. One day it seems to be the vanguard of the fight with Satan, and on the next it has taken a place amongst the rearguard; though perhaps it would be more true to say that it was both, since the royal prophet, who tells us how God's mercy went before him, also assures us that it followed him all the days of his life. But apart from all these ways of considering the work of grace, there is another division, by far the most important of all, and assuredly the most famous, for when we say that grace is either sufficient or efficacious, we open up questions that have been debated in the schools for hundreds of years; and as it is essential for the right understanding of our subject that we should go into this division more completely, we had better begin by explaining our terms.

It is not quite correct to say that by "sufficiency" we mean to signify the exact opposite of what is insufficient or deficient in any way, for when we come to analyze the word we find that it is capable of conveying two distinct significations. We call a power "sufficient" if we know it to be capable of producing its peculiar effect, without reference to or dependence on any other object; and on the other hand we should be justified in speaking of an agent as "sufficient" in its own order, although we know that actually to produce the result desired, it necessarily depended on the correspondence of an agent in some other order. So a railway company may build a perfect locomotive, and yet its work would be a failure were the coal supply to be exhausted, or the rails on which it runs to be in any way imperfect. When we speak of "sufficient" grace, it is in this latter sense that we are using the word, for we simply mean that it is all that is desired or required to give the will the power to act. You cannot justly say therefore that we are playing with words, and that a given power is not sufficient, if something else be necessary to produce the right effect. There is all the difference in the world between an actual reality, and mere possibility. The power is sufficient, if it make the effect possible—the actual production of the effect is quite another question. So the sunshine pours itself upon the garden beds all moistened with the warm spring rain; and yet it happens that a certain plant will make no progress, but withers in its bloom. There was sufficient sunshine, and sufficient rain—the cause of failure must be sought elsewhere.

On the other hand, we call that cause or power efficacious which is not only quite incapable of failure in itself, but likewise quite incapable of being checked by others, which meets resistance only to overcome it, and so conquers all possible obstacles that the effect is infallibly certain. Bearing this in mind, we can turn to the many definitions and explanations of sufficient and efficacious grace that have been used by writers on these subjects, and their meaning is at once apparent.

Sufficient grace, they say, will give us power to do a good work, and efficacious grace will add the good use of that same power; sufficient grace enables us to do an act of virtue if we wish it; efficacious grace will make us wish it. Sufficient grace, says St. Augustine, is the help without which we cannot succeed, efficacious grace the help by which we actually do succeed. The one is part of that ordinary providence which ordains things to a certain end, and gives to each sufficient means to carry out that end, without, however, taking away or neutralizing those defects which may prevent success; the other belongs rather to that special providence of God which so arranges ways and means, that final success is absolutely certain, even though failure always remains possible.

We have not time to go into this question with anything like the fullness it deserves. We can only briefly state the teaching of the first and greatest of the Church's doctors, and of that school whose proudest glory is the possession of his name. According to St. Thomas and the Thomists, therefore, grace is either sufficient or efficacious. Sufficient grace, we hold, is given to all, and efficacious grace to many—both sufficient grace and efficacious grace are absolutely gratuitous; and finally—and here is the stumbling block of the Thomistic system, according to its opponents—efficacious grace is efficacious *because of the Almighty Will of God*; it derives its efficiency from Him and from Him alone, and it is hardly necessary to add that we hold that this power of grace is in no way opposed to man's free will, or liberty. Let us examine these propositions more closely.

First of all, with regard to sufficient grace. It signified, we said, a grace which bestows the power to do a good work. God most certainly does bestow such graces. They are not to be seen so much in this or that particular act on the part of God, as in a series of blessings and favors of every sort which Providence pours upon each soul according to its own particular need, strengthening it and helping it in every way, so that if it fail to attain the end for which it was created, the failure is not through want of power or ability, but simply through want of good will. How frequently and how vividly does God put this before us in His inspired Scriptures? "Behold," He says in the Book of Revelation (Rev. 3:20), "I stand at the door and knock: if any man will open unto me, I will come in to him;" and on that most startling occasion when our Lord so vehemently denounced the Scribes and Pharisees, the denunciation changes in the end to a cry of loving sorrow, and shows us that the cause of His anger and His sorrow was the sight of all the graces offered to that stiff-necked people and rejected by them. "How often," He said, "how often would I have gathered your children to my breast, as the bird does her brood under her wings, and you would not" (Matt. 23:37; Luke 13:34). But nowhere is this more clearly put before us than in the fifth chapter of Isaiah, where the familiar figure of a vineyard is made use of by the prophet. Here we see, in the various efforts of the husbandman, a picture of the abundant graces bestowed by God upon the souls He has made, varying indeed according to the varying circumstances and needs of each, yet always sufficient for the work to which they are called. Thus, as we have already pointed out in the beginning of this chapter, God would have us see in the ordinary events of life, the beckoning of His hand; in the many beauties of nature, the reflection of His uncreated loveliness; in the order and symmetry of the universe, the silent worship of its great Creator. He would have us see and hear in all created things, a gracious invitation from on high, calling upon us likewise to glorify our God. In addition to this outward appeal, God speaks to the heart of man by those natural virtues and inclinations towards good, which even our weak sight can see so plainly, as well as by those passing lights and shadows and caressing blessings which so often stir the coldest heart, and tell it God is nigh. And because He is the Master and Supreme Ruler of all, it is within His power to change and move the will of man, as well as to attract it or repel it by contrasted pictures of good and evil and their necessary fruits. Then, again, we feel how differently the grace of God will act upon a soul that has received the grace of baptism, and one that has not been so blessed. In the one, the habits of faith and hope and love are there to welcome every touch of grace, though it may be but the faintest; whereas the other soul is plunged in darkness, and the grace that comes to it would be a glimmer of light to make it see the misery of its state, and lead it on to work for something better. Both might be called sufficient graces; but in the one case theologians would say it was "remote," whereas the grace that finds the soul already prepared is "proximate." So also the habitual sinner who never thinks of God, or of the misery of his state, could hardly be said to have a proximate sufficient grace to change his life, but he most certainly has at his disposal that remote sufficient grace which would enable him to realize his wretchedness and beg the help that will not be denied.

This leads us naturally to ask if sufficient grace of some sort or another is really given to all—a question frequently put forward and denied by unbelieving writers. It is, in truth, a serious and important question, and one which touches most directly on the judgments of Almighty God, which, St. Paul warns us, are as incomprehensible as His ways are unsearchable, and to which, therefore, we must reply with all diffidence and most humble reverence. And this is what we venture to put forward as our answer. No one on earth, however wicked he may be, is so abandoned by Almighty God as not to have at least that help and grace, remote it may be, yet truly sufficient, which would enable him to turn from sin, or keep the law of God in this or that particular instance. So, in the case of pagans and unbelievers, we should say that there is no one who, at some time or other, does not receive that help from God which, if accepted, would prove the harbinger of mightier graces leading him to know and love and serve his Maker. It is an axiom amongst us: grace is never denied to those who do their best. "We believe most firmly," says St. Augustine, "that God, who is so good and just, could not command what is impossible, and hence He shows us what to do in easy things, and what to ask for in those that are more difficult."

We now pass on to efficacious grace; and though we have already said what we mean by it, and whence, according to St. Thomas and his school, it derives its infallible efficiency, we may be pardoned if we try to give a fuller explanation, since this is just the one great difficulty to the opponents of Thomistic doctrine. The word efficacious, when applied to grace, necessarily includes the idea of final success. We sometimes speak of a remedy as efficacious because it is very powerful, and usually produces the effect desired, though it may fail in this or that particular instance. But by efficacious grace we mean a grace which infallibly produces its effect, a grace which never fails; and that Almighty God does sometimes give such graces is clearly and repeatedly asserted by the Holy Scriptures, and therefore is not denied by any Catholic theologian. The controversies in the Catholic schools during the past three hundred years have been waged over the further question: what makes this grace so sure and so infallible, and the reply so unanimously and so emphatically given by St. Thomas and his followers: The Almighty Will of God!

The new opinions which were first put forward in the sixteenth century were a praiseworthy endeavor to throw further light on what is, and ever must be, a wondrous mystery. We have spoken of them in the first chapter, and we shall have to allude to them again in our last, for the difficulty with which we are now face to face is not a new difficulty. Whether it be the question of free will, or efficacious grace, or predestination, the mystery is ever the same, the difficulty is ever the same—God's omnipotence in contact with man's freedom—and the solution offered by the first and greatest of the Catholic schools is ever the same also—in fact, it is the only solution offered by a school, for the opposing theories are the suggestions of individuals. The Thomists, therefore, attribute the efficiency of grace to the Almighty Will of God, and to that supreme and absolute dominion which He exercises over our free will as over any other created thing, so that the infallible connection between a grace and its effect is based, not simply on God's infinite knowledge but on His causality. The result is infallibly certain, not because God knows we shall consent, but because He wills it, and therefore brings it about, and could not know it otherwise. There are two most certain principles which are the basis of this doctrine, and which seem to make it as certain as anything can be certain which is not a dogma of faith, and they are these: To consent to grace and to do what is right is most certainly a good effect, whereas to dissent from grace, and to do evil is manifestly a defect; for St. Thomas lays it down as an axiom, that whatever failure there may be in any action is due to the defect of some principle.[3] But, as you may perhaps remember, we asserted in the first chapter, that everything which is good, and everything which has being, must be attributed to the efficiency of God, the First great Cause, and any defect that there may be is the work of the second cause. For God is the First efficient Cause of all being and all good, the second cause is the occasion of failure; not that God makes it so, but that, being made out of nothing, its efficiency is limited and capable of failure. Therefore, no matter what theory you may adopt, you must come back to this at last: grace sometimes fails in its effect because of us, and when it succeeds its success is due to God. The First Being is the principle of all being; the First Good is the fountain and source of all good; the First Cause is the cause of every effect and of the causality of second causes. We cannot deny these principles, and it is folly to shirk them simply because it seems hard to reconcile them to our idea of liberty. In the first chapter we tried to show how God moved the will without interfering with its freedom. We showed that God's

3. *ST* I, q. 49, a. 1.

omnipotence is as universal as it is efficient, and that it must extend to all beings, and all the most minute differences and modes of being, otherwise He is not God. The action of His causality, therefore, is efficient in every way, and gives being not only to the action itself, but to its mode as well, so that it is in accordance with the nature of the agent which produces it. Hence, if it be a necessary cause, God makes it act necessarily; if it be a free cause, He makes it act freely, and in no way destroys its indifference to that particular act, and its freedom to do the opposite. The divine motion of which we are speaking does not give the power of acting or not acting; it supposes it already given; and when the act is being brought about, the power to do the opposite remains untouched, and in that lies the essence of liberty.

We have nothing further to say on this matter. It is enough, surely, and more than enough, to make us realize the exceeding importance of trying to estimate our grace at its true value. It is enough, and more than enough, to make us understand something of what is meant by working out our salvation with fear and trembling. There are such things as comfortable and easy theories, comfortable and easy explanations of the dread mysteries of God, but they cannot make the work of salvation easy and comfortable to a careless soul, they cannot do away with the fear and trembling. "You cannot manufacture another God," says a spiritual writer, "you must take Him as you find Him;" and then, contemplating the action of grace on our souls, the same writer goes on to draw this brief conclusion, a conclusion eminently fitted to our own subject: "It is an extremely serious thing to have to do with God."

V

The Cause of Grace

We have now to treat of the cause of grace, and before attempting to lay down any proposition on this subject it would be well to define our terms, and so obviate the danger of any misconception. It is easy enough to talk about causes and causality, but it is not so easy to express the precise ideas these words are meant to convey. If we take for granted that a "principle" is that from which anything proceeds, we might define a cause as a principle which by its influence determines the existence of anything else; but, even with this definition, there still remains a great deal to be said by way of explanation before we can proceed with our subject. Suppose an artist wishes to paint a picture or carve a statue, we see at once that there are many influences which may affect the result of his work. The man himself has to be considered, the idea in his mind, the materials or instruments he has at his disposal, the person or persons for whom he works, the end he has in view: all these things are so many "principles" to be taken into account, since by their influence they most certainly determine the existence of the picture or statue in question. So the old schoolmen wisely classified causes as final or efficient, formal or material,[1] and the distinction is as necessary as it is wise. A certain writer, whose learning was in truth a dangerous thing because so very little, once ventured to put forward, as an argument in favor of evolution, that it was in every way a nobler thing for man to be developed from the living organism of a monkey, than from the lifeless clod of earth. To many it certainly might seem so, but we may perhaps be pardoned if we hold that to be formed by a monkey from a monkey is in every way less honorable to man, than to be formed from the earth by the great Creator Himself. It is, in other words, a question of causes. In the one case, the monkey is the efficient cause as well as the material cause; but in the other, the earth is the material cause, and the efficient cause is the Almighty Power of God. So when we talk about the cause of grace, our duty first of all is manifestly to explain which cause we mean. What is the final cause of grace, the end for which it is bestowed upon us? The Word of God has left us here no room for doubt or hesitation. "The water which I will give," said our Lord to the Samaritan woman, "shall be a well of water springing up into everlasting life." The final cause of grace is our salvation, and our salvation is for the glory of God, as St. Paul so wisely, yet so eloquently, declares: "All things are yours, and you are Christ's, and Christ is God's" (1 Cor. 3:22).

1.

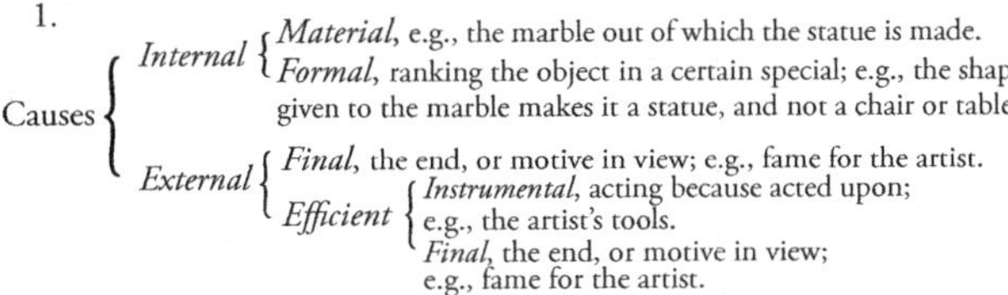

From what we have already said about the nature of grace, it will be seen at once that, strictly speaking, it can have no formal cause, and we may call the essence of the soul its material cause, since there it is that grace abides when all has been prepared by fitting dispositions, of which we must say more in the course of this chapter. The real question at issue, therefore, is with reference to the principal efficient cause of grace, and to this question the Angelic Doctor briefly answers that God and God alone can be the cause of grace, according to the words of Holy Scripture, "The Lord gives grace and glory" (Ps. 84). So also in the prophets we hear God declaring to the children of Israel that He alone is God, and there is "no other Savior" (Is. 43:25), "I, even I," He says, "am He that blotted out your transgressions for my own sake" (Hos. 13:4), and hence St. Augustine asserts that the bestowal of grace is a positive proof of the Divinity. "He who can dare to say, I justify you, can also say, believe in me; and therefore no one, no matter how holy he may be, can dare to use such words or claim such powers—no one save the Holy of holies Himself." And this surely requires no proof. Recall what we have said about the nature of this gift of God, remember the strange words of St. Peter, describing it as nothing less than a participation of the divine Nature. Try to realize all that is meant by being adopted of God, called to share in His infinite riches and to be associated in the everlasting glory of His happiness, being made heirs of His Kingdom.[2] Think of the victory over sin, and the consequent consecration of the soul as the temple of the Holy Spirit—and then ask yourselves, with David, "Who has wrought all these things?", and you will anticipate the inspired answer:

2. *ST* III, q. 23, a. 1.

"Who but I, the Lord?" For who can carry out a supernatural work but He who is the Maker and the Lord of all? Who can make poor mortals partakers of the divine Nature but He in whom resides the fullness of the Godhead? Who can give the adoption of sons, and make us heirs to the inheritance, but He who is at once Father and Lord? Who can forgive sins but He whom sin has outraged, the God of all holiness? Who can send down the Holy Spirit into our hearts but the Infinite, adorable Trinity—the co-equal and inseparable Persons who send and are sent in that they give themselves, Father, Son, and Holy Spirit, three in one, and one in three—one essence, one substance—one God!

But, you might object, granting all this, granting that God and God alone can be the efficient cause of grace in such a way that He alone can give it by His own intrinsic right, a right of nature, can we not suppose that in His goodness He may bestow the right on others, and allow them as a favor to exercise a power which in itself is His alone? The very fact that grace is what it is, the height to which it raises us, "low-born clods of brute earth" though we may be, seems to justify us in supposing that such a miracle of condescension on the part of God is not impossible. If we are partakers of the divine Nature, may we not be made partakers of the divine Power? And does not the Church itself seem to admit that some such privilege was conferred on her who was the sinless Mother of the world's Redeemer, our "tainted nature's solitary boast," when it speaks of her as Mother of divine Grace? No, says St. Thomas, it is impossible! We are indeed partakers of the divine Nature, in that we enjoy a happiness which belongs to the Divinity, but not that we can claim the Godhead as our own. Because we are adopted sons, we cannot possibly transmit to others what we have been allowed by privilege to share—nay, our very nature forbids it, for grace, as we have seen, affects the inmost soul of man, and even acts upon his will; and the power to change our souls and influence our wills is the inalienable attribute of God alone. And what has been said of Mary the Virgin Mother of our Savior, so exalted in her grandeur, so beautiful in her purity, will serve to lead us on to our next point, for she is what she is because she is the Mother of Christ, God made man for us. We call her Mother of divine Grace, because she was chosen to minister to the Eternal Word, the Body and Blood of His earthly tabernacle, and Holy Scripture tells us plainly that "grace and truth came by Jesus Christ," and of "His fullness we have all received" (John 1:16–17).

Jesus Christ, then, is also the cause of our grace; let us see how this is so. Our Blessed Lord was God and man, "perfect God and perfect man, with a rational soul, and a human body," as the Athanasian Creed declares. As God, therefore, He certainly was, according to what has been already said, the efficient cause of grace; but His humanity had a work to do as well, for, as St. Thomas goes on to say, His human nature was, so to speak, "the instrument of His Godhead,"[3] and when an instrument does anything, it is not by its own power, but by the power of him who uses it. Hence the actions of our Blessed Lord acquire an infinite value from His divine nature, being the actions of God incarnate. To understand this more clearly, we must go back a little on our doctrine of causes, and our example of the artist or sculptor. As we watch him at work, we are obliged to say that, by his own power, and by a real influence, he is producing a certain result, and as we notice the touches of the brush or the strokes of the

3. *ST* I-II, q. 112, a. 1, ad 1.

chisel, we must admit also that those instruments have communicated to them, for the time being, some of his power and energy. Both the artist and his tools are causes, efficient causes and physical causes; but whereas the one is really and truly the principal cause, the other is but instrumental.[4] Or, to take another example, when Queen Philippa pleaded for the townsmen of Calais, it was her worth, her dignity, and the affection which he had for her, which made King Edward spare them. We should call her therefore the principal moral cause of their deliverance, and had she pleaded by letter instead of in person, her letter might be called the moral instrumental cause of the same act of clemency. The action of a cause may therefore be either physical or moral, and in each case the cause itself may be principal or merely instrumental; and with this before our eyes, we may ask ourselves in what way, or in how many ways, was our Blessed Lord and Savior the cause of our grace and our salvation? In every way! That is the true answer.

For it is only "through Jesus Christ our Lord," as the Church so often reminds us, that we dare to hope for grace and that salvation which is its fruit. It was He who blotted out the handwriting that was against us, and he did this, in the graphic words of the Apostle, by nailing it to the cross on which He died. He it was who loved us so dearly that He washed us from our sins in His own Blood (Rev. 1:5). So St. Thomas,[5] summing up a series of most beautiful articles on the passion of our Savior, points out this distinction of

4. Cf. note p. 195. 5. A "moral" cause would seem to be reducible to the class of final causes, since its effect is not produced by actual contact, but by its influence on the efficient cause.

5. *ST* III, qq. 48–49.

causes to which we have alluded, and then goes on to say that God is the principal efficient cause of our salvation, and Jesus Christ is God. And because His most sacred humanity was the instrument of the Divinity, all his actions and sufferings were the instrumental means by which the great work was brought about. He is also the principal moral cause of all our graces, because these actions and sufferings were meritorious, inasmuch as they were freely accepted and most lovingly endured by His human will. And if we look at these same sufferings as endured in His adorable body, we shall see how the work was done. Because of the greatness of His love, and the unspeakable dignity of His divine Person, as well as because of the multitude of His sufferings, an atonement that was in every way most superabundant was offered to God's justice. Because His Blood as shed in death was the price of this atonement, and He paid it with such lavish generosity, He, and He alone, is our Redeemer; and lastly, inasmuch as the voluntary sacrifice of His life was the most perfect act of worship that could be given to God, it is by His death—the death of the Son of God—that the world is reconciled to its Creator. What a significance is given by thoughts like these to that eloquent cry of St. Paul: "Blessed be God, the Father of our Lord Jesus Christ, who has blessed us with all spiritual blessings in Christ" (Eph. 1:8).

But now, passing from the thought of all these countless graces and blessings that have come to the world through the life and death of Jesus our Savior, we must go on to consider for a moment those definite channels of grace so familiar to us all—the Seven Sacraments. In our Blessed Lord we seem to see the manifest working of the awful power of grace, for virtue went out from Him for the healing of all; but in the Sacraments that same almighty power lies hidden and concealed, and so St. Thomas describes them as most sacred things in which the divine virtue operates salvation secretly. For the Sacraments are causes of grace. They have their efficacy from the Incarnate Word, and the Angelic Doctor compares them to an instrument used by the Sacred Humanity. He uses the homely comparison of a stick held in the hand. Both hand and stick are instruments, but the hand is actually joined to the source of motion, while the stick is separate, and owes its motion entirely to the hand. So, he says,[6] the Sacred Humanity is joined to the Godhead, which is the efficient cause of grace, and the saving virtue of Christ's Divinity passes to the Sacraments through His humanity. The Sacraments, therefore, carry on the work of the passion, freeing us from sin, and helping us to draw nearer to God by the practice of virtue. And how do they do this? How do the Sacraments cause grace? Before replying to this question, we must lay down a simple, but very necessary distinction, which is frequently misunderstood by non-Catholics—the distinction between the production of grace *ex opere operantis* and *ex opera operato*, which is only another way of saying that grace may be given out of deference to the person who is acting, or because of the act he is doing. Grace is given *ex opere operantis* when God bestows it because of the goodness and fervor of the soul which is doing something for Him; but when, on the contrary, He does not regard the soul so much as the action which it is performing, and which in this instance is an act instituted by His only begotten Son for the purpose of producing grace, then the grace is said to be given *ex opere operato*.

The Sacraments, then, give grace *ex opere operato*; they are the instrumental causes of grace. But when we have said

6. *ST* III, q. 62, a. 5.

this we are face to face with another question, which once again throws us back on our distinctions: Are they the physical instruments of grace, or is their efficiency limited to what we called moral? The Church has defined nothing, and the various schools hold various opinions. All admit them to be moral instrumental causes at the very least, for Jesus Christ is, as we have said, the principal moral cause or meritorious cause of grace, and the merits of His passion and death are in the Sacraments; He has willed that whenever the Sacraments are rightly administered, the effect is the same as though His passion and death were once more offered to His Eternal Father. But the Thomist school goes further and unanimously teaches that the Sacraments are the instrumental causes of grace, not only morally, but also physically; and this seems to be the opinion of many theologians not of the Thomist school. St. Thomas boldly compares them to tools in the hands of the carpenter, and says that God makes use of them in a similar way to be the physical instruments of grace for the souls of men. And most wonderful instruments they are! All alike in that they are divine instruments, and yet entirely different in their mode of operation—some absolutely necessary, some accidentally necessary, some only desirable; and so matter, which seems in every way the farthest removed from, the most opposed to, that spiritual supernatural world in which God dwells, becomes in His hands the most mighty weapon of the most supernatural of all His works.

To pass on to another point, we said in the beginning of this chapter that we must look upon the material cause of grace as those dispositions of the soul which dispose it to be the fitting theater of all these wonders. Of course it is quite evident that an actual grace from God need not suppose any preparation, since it is often bestowed upon the greatest sinners, and indeed is in itself a preparation for greater blessings yet to come. But we are speaking of the gift of habitual sanctifying grace such as is poured upon the soul in Holy Baptism or at the moment of sincere repentance after sin. And for this, St. Thomas holds,[7] there must be some sort of preparation; not that God, who is infinite in power depends for His success upon the previous work of some secondary cause, but that being also infinite in wisdom, it is only fitting that His works should proceed in due order, and therefore, before acting on any of His creatures or using them in any way, He Himself should bring to pass the necessary or fitting conditions.

So with regard to those who turn to Him after yielding to sin, it is a dogma of our faith that there should be this conversion, or turning of the will to God before He gives His grace. "Turn ye to me," He says "and I will turn to you" (Zach. 1:3), and therefore the Council of Trent[8] anathematizes those who dare to hold the contrary and the reason of this is very clear since God always acts in accordance with our nature. Grace does not force nature or destroy it, but perfects it in every way and hence, when God pours in His grace, He at the same time moves the will to accept it freely. But remember this conversion of the will to God, this repentance is not the efficient cause of the grace that is given—it only disposes the soul to receive it. In the case of little children, we cannot say, of course, that this disposition is in their souls by their own act, since they are not yet capable of reason or free will; but as the Holy Fathers so beautifully say, God takes for granted in them what they certainly cannot

7. *ST* II-II, q. 6, a. 1.
8. Council of Trent, Session VI, ch. 16, Canons 7 and 9.

deny or refuse and our Holy Mother the Church speaks for them giving them a heart that they may believe unto justice and a mouth to confess their faith unto salvation. Now you may ask this most important question: Suppose a man really and truly tries his best to have these dispositions, is he certain to receive grace? It is a question which was more or less replied to in the last chapter, when, touching on the case of heathens and unbelievers, we asserted that there was no one, who, at some time or other, does not receive that help, which, if welcomed by the soul, would surely bring down further help and more abundant blessings. But the question we are asking now goes farther—it is a question of cause and effect. Suppose a man puts himself in these dispositions, is the consequent supply of grace infallibly certain? To this we reply that no mere natural act can infallibly bring grace. A life that never goes beyond the powers of nature can never justly claim a supernatural reward, otherwise the first step in the work of our salvation would be our own, and not the effect of grace, as our Faith teaches. But if a man acts up to his lights, and with God's help really and truly puts himself in God's hands, and humbly seeks to do His will, then most infallibly will grace be given to him to show him what God's will in his regard may be.

Then, finally, since the certainty of an effect depends upon our knowledge of the cause, we may ask if it is possible to feel quite certain that we ourselves possess this glorious gift of grace. One of the many strange, unreasonable theories held by those outside the Catholic Church is concerned with this very question, for there are some who hold that man not only can, but must, feel certain that his sins are all forgiven and that he enjoys God's grace. They hold that this strange certitude is like an article of faith, an indispensable condition of salvation. But the Catholic Church would have us look on this as nothing less than wild presumption, for she teaches that, without a special revelation, no one could claim a certitude of such a nature, equivalent as it is to an act of faith. The only certitude we can enjoy is moral certitude, a certainty which is based on strong convincing reasons, and which is a sufficient guide for all the ordinary duties of our lives. The reasons which we must look for in our hearts to assure us of our grace are fully mentioned by the Angelic Doctor.[9] We give them as a practical conclusion. First of all, a real love for the things of God. This includes devout and frequent use of the Sacraments, the divinely appointed means of grace; the practice of prayer, which keeps the soul habitually at God's feet; good reading, sermons, and instructions. "He that is of God"—notice the words—"hears the words of God" (John 8:47). In the next place, detachment from worldly things. This does not mean renunciation or heroic sacrifice, but a commonsense view of life and duty, which prevents us fixing our hearts on what is unworthy of them. In the third place, as a natural consequence of this detachment, the adherence of the will to God and the hearty avoidance of sin and all that tears us from Him; and, lastly, a real, true, sincere distrust of self, and a slowness to assume the role of judging others. What is all this, but working out our salvation, with fear and trembling?

9. *ST* I-II, q. 112, a. 5.

VI

Grace and the Sinner

After considering in the last chapter the causes of grace, we now naturally pass on to the study of its effects, and the wonderful consequences of its presence in the soul, the justification of the sinner, the merit of our good works, and, finally, that heavenly glory which is at once the beginning and the end, the final cause of our grace as well as its everlasting reward. For before we can be allowed to gaze upon the unveiled beauty of God's Face, before our poor works can in any way be worthy of such high recompense, grace must render us pleasing in God's sight: it must anticipate us with its many blessings of sweetness (Ps. 20), placing upon our heads its crown of precious stones, and this we call justification. It is certainly one of the most beautiful works of God, and as such is in every way worthy of our study, and our most diligent contemplation. Compare it with other great works of God, other manifestations of His love for His creatures, and it loses nothing by the comparison. We think of the act of creation or the glorification of God's elect, yet St. Thomas does not shrink from declaring that the justification of a soul is His greatest work.[1] It is the divine fruit of the Incarnation, which it necessarily supposes. And though perhaps our imagination may picture the act of creation as more wonderful, since it implies the production of existence out of nothing, yet our reason will reply that justification is yet more wonderful, since it has to overcome the opposition of the corrupt will of man. "He who made you without your help," says St. Augustine, "will not justify you without it," and in another place, the same holy Doctor says that to make a bad man good is a greater work than the creation of heaven and earth, for the end of creation is but a man's natural good, existence, whereas justification effects a good which is supernatural, everlasting life. So, also, at first sight the gift of glory seems a greater gift than justifying grace; but, after all, glory is bestowed on one who has deserved it, and labored for it as his reward, while justifying grace must act upon a sinner who merits naught but chastisement. Most justly, then, does Holy Scripture say that God's mercies are above all His works; and the Church, following up the same idea, glorifies that God, whose power is principally shown in His loving pity and condescending mercy.[2]

We are considering justification, in this chapter, in its most limited sense as that act of divine power by which a soul stained with the guilt of sin is once more purified and rendered pleasing in His sight. Hence the whole question naturally supposes a knowledge of the nature of sin and its baleful effects on the soul; and to put it more vividly before us we may once more turn to one of the parables of our

1. *ST* I-II, q. 113, a. 9.
2. *Deus qui omnipotentiam tuam parcendo maxime et miserando manifestas* (Collect, Tenth Sunday after Pentecost).

Blessed Lord and let it help us in our explanation. It is the familiar parable of the Pharisee and the Publican (Luke 18). Two men, says our Lord, went up to the Temple to pray. One of them was a Pharisee, a man eminently respectable in every way, as far as this world judges, and his prayer was a foolish and useless proclamation of his own imaginary virtues, an insincere profession of gratitude that he was not as bad as the rest of men. Our Lord does not condescend to tell us that his prayer was rejected, nor was it necessary: we feel that it could not be otherwise. There was no welcome for him, no blessing for him, because of his pride and self-conceit. And the other man, who stood afar off, and hardly dared to raise his eyes to heaven, was one who was despised by all because of his publicly sinful life. He lived by the unjust oppression of others; he was therefore in sin, grievous sin, and the weight of God's anger was heavy on his soul. He was the slave of the devil, bound down by chains of his own forging. In his will was the seed of eternal aversion from God, and that everlasting hell which is its necessary fruit. And so he came up to the Temple of God, and perhaps the sight of its magnificence awakened in his heart some thoughts of that great Creator whom he had lived to despise. At all events, grace touched him, faith awakened, and his soul at once opened to drink in the saving light. He saw his misery, his sinfulness, and a great fear of God's judgments fell upon him. Yet, even as he feared, hope came to comfort him, and love followed hope, and "perfect love casts out fear," or rather transforms it into deeper contrition. "God," he prayed, "God, be merciful to me, a sinner!" and the work was done. No one but God heard the whispered words, but they were enough for the accomplishment of this most glorious of the divine works. "Amen, I say unto you, that man went down to his house justified." God spoke the word, and life came back to that soul that was dead in sin. Grace, the source and principle of all supernatural life, was once more quickening and vivifying its understanding and its will. Faith and hope and charity had on the instant clothed it with a robe of beauty, and sin was as though it had never been, and the Holy of Holies itself, hidden there behind the Veil of the Temple, was not holier than the soul of that poor publican, for in it, as in the Holy of Holies, dwelt the Eternal Majesty of God. "Amen, I say unto you, that man went down to his house justified." Truly a wonderful change—so wonderful that, as St. Peter Chrysologus says, "the angels are astonished, heaven marvels, earth trembles, flesh cannot bear it, ears cannot take it in, the mind cannot grasp it, the whole creation is too weak to endure its magnitude and short of intellect to esteem it rightly and afraid of believing it because it is so much." And it is this wonderful work of justification that we want to consider.

In the third chapter, when speaking of the nature of grace, we alluded to the teaching of those who see in grace nothing more than "imputing" to the sinner the merits of Christ. According to them there is no interior change, no destruction of the work of sin; on the contrary, they would have us believe that it remains in all its horror, though covered by the merits of our Savior, so that justification on God's side would consist in overlooking the sin because of Christ's merits, and on the part of the sinner in firmly believing that all the sins of the past, and those of the future as well, are already condoned and effectually hidden—so condoned and so hidden that damnation becomes impossible. Certainly a very comfortable doctrine, but one which is subversive of the most ordinary morality. The Catholic teaching, on the contrary, commands us to believe that when justifying grace is bestowed upon a soul, the stains of sin that may be there are not merely covered over, but effectually destroyed and blotted out. It surely needs no proof to convince us that sin is a stain upon the soul! What says our Blessed Lord? "Evil thoughts, murders, impurities: these are the things that defile a man" (Matt. 15:19). And at the moment of our Baptism, when the priest had poured upon our heads the cleansing waters of Baptism, and clothed us with the robe of grace, he bestowed upon us the outward emblem of the sacred rite with words that remind us of this same truth. "Receive this white garment," he said, "and see that you carry it without stain before the judgment seat of our Lord Jesus Christ." Every sin that the soul commits in after years is a stain upon that white garment.[3] For the bright whiteness of the soul has a double origin—the shining light of natural reason, and the dazzling glory of God's grace. And when the soul, in defiance of the dictates of its reason, cleaves to what is vile and loathsome, then is its brightness dimmed and sometimes wholly destroyed. And until the will forsakes the evil which it has embraced and returns to the one true Good whom it has abandoned, that dark stain rests upon it and defiles it in the sight of heaven. So when in Holy Scripture God promises to His repentant people the grace of forgiveness, it is always a cleansing from stains which He offers them. "I will pour out upon you," He says, "clean water, and you shall be made clean from all your filthiness" (Ez. 36:25). And again, "I, even I, am He that blots out your transgressions" (Is. 43:25). It is always this same cleansing that is besought so earnestly in the prayers He Himself has placed upon the lips of His inspired servants, and nowhere more touchingly than in the

3. *ST* I-II, q. 86, aa. 1–2.

fifty-first Psalm—the first and best of all acts of contrition and repentance. "Have mercy on me, O God, according to Your great mercy, and according to the multitude of Your tender mercies blot out my iniquity. Wash me yet more from my iniquity, and cleanse me from my sin... You shall sprinkle me as a leper, and I shall be made clean; You shall wash me, and I shall be made whiter than snow." And the same beautiful idea is put before us by the beloved disciple when he speaks of the means of our purification. "Jesus Christ," he says, "who has loved us, and washed us from our sins in His own Blood" (Rev. 1:5).

Manifestly, then, the work of grace is a real purification of the soul and not a mere covering up of our sinfulness. The nature of grace makes such a theory impossible. For this divine gift is, as we said before, an outpouring of God's love upon His creatures, and therefore it implies a real internal change of heart since the almighty love of God cannot be mistaken, but must necessarily effect and produce in its object the particular perfection in which it takes delight. It is quite true that even after justifying grace has put an end to sin, concupiscence remains, and in this unhappy consequence of our fallen state, this tendency and inclination towards sin which lingers in the soul that has been born again to Christ, the opponents of the Catholic doctrine tried to see a proof of their own theories, and urged that this was sin according to St. Paul; but the great Council of Trent refused to see this meaning in the Apostle's words, and declared that though concupiscence remained in those who are baptized, and though it is the fruit of sin, as well as its most dangerous occasion, yet it remains but for the greater trial and perfection of God's faithful servants, in nowise turning Him against them as long as they resisted manfully. "There is no condemnation," says St. Paul, and therefore no sin, "to them that are in Christ Jesus;" and he gives the reason: "since they walk not according to the flesh… for if we live according to the flesh we shall die; but if by the Spirit we mortify the deeds of the flesh, we shall live" (Rom. 8:1, 4, 13). The grace of justification, then, is the utter destruction of sin. Let us look at the mystery still more closely, and try to see how the wonderful work is done.

All Catholics believe that when the act of justification takes place, and sin is blotted out from the soul, grace falls like a heavenly dew upon the dry and thirsty land, so that where iniquity abounded, grace now abounds. All Catholics admit this, and it has been defined in the Council of Trent. "If any one shall say that man is justified only by the remission of sins, and without any outpouring of the Holy Spirit, diffusing grace and love in His heart—let such a one be anathema."[4] But, while admitting that this is always the fact, we may ask ourselves if God could possibly justify a sinner without infusing grace, for our reply to the question will help us greatly to understand the work of justification. Of course, the very act of forgiveness must be looked upon as a grace in itself, for it is certainly no small favor or grace that God should forgive His rebellious creature and admit him to the blessings of His friendship. But, as we have so often pointed out, grace is a word of many meanings, and so some have thought that God can, absolutely speaking, forgive and remit sin by a purely external act of forgiveness, without at the same time bestowing any internal favor on the sinner; others, leaving out of question what God can do or cannot do by His absolute power, consider that justification is actually

4. Council of Trent, Session 6, ch. 16, Canon 11.

effected by the love and sorrow in the sinner's heart, under the influence of a special help from God. But the common opinion holds that, by the act of justification, not only is the sin remitted, but the soul is raised to the supernatural state, and indeed, that justification cannot take place without this outpouring of supernatural blessings and favors.

The first opinion seems to us impossible, because founded on a misconception. Its advocates seem to think that sin is nothing but the infringement of a penal law, subjecting the offender to a certain penalty and nothing more, and hence they argue that if God remit the penalty, the work is done. But surely sin, according to the Catholic idea, is something more than that. Sin is the rejection of Almighty God, our last end even as He is our first beginning, and the choice of some created pleasure in His place. Sin is the willful spurning of God's grace and friendship and the insult which such contemptuous treatment necessarily implies. The act of sin is therefore something far more than the mere liability to a penalty. It deforms and sullies the gracious handiwork of God and makes it odious in His sight and deserving of His anger. And we fail to see how all this can be undone by any mere external condonation, any more than a costly vase, which a reckless blow has shivered into fragments, can be replaced upon its stand by excusing the offender. Such a condonation on the part of God would not imply necessarily that the sinner had returned to Him and fallen at His feet and craved forgiveness with true repentant love. This comparison suggests our answer to those who hold the second opinion we spoke of—who would see in justification nothing more than this repentance and true sorrow on the part of the rebellious soul. It does not go far enough. It does not prove the reinstatement of the prodigal son. It says nothing of the loving welcome from his father, the eager bestowal of the best robe, and the ring of sonship—and yet surely this is what we mean by justification; for though the act of sin itself is momentary and may easily be forgotten, its effects continue, and it is really and truly a sad departure from our Father's house, an obstinate, willful tarrying in a far-off land.

We hold, then, that justification means sanctification, or, to use the words of the Council of Vienna, the "renovation of the interior man by the infusion of sanctifying grace, and its consequent blessings," and so by justification, as the same Council goes on to say so beautifully, the sinful soul becomes holy, the enemy of God becomes His friend, and heir to everlasting glory. And St. Thomas naturally teaches the same.[5] The forgiveness of sin, he says, would be altogether unintelligible, unless at the same time the soul of the forgiven sinner were filled with sanctifying grace. For sin is an offense against God, a declaration of war against Him, and reconciliation means nothing less than restoration to love and friendship. And the token and pledge of this love is the presence of sanctifying grace in the soul. Surely we begin to see now why the Angelic Doctor ventures to conclude his treatise on this subject by declaring justification to be the greatest work of God, and we begin, too, to have some faint and far off glimpse of all the wondrous miracles of power and pity, summed up in those brief words of our Savior—"That man went down to his house justified" (Luke 18:14).

Now we may go on to consider briefly the dispositions which prepare the soul to be the theater of these wonders. From the teaching of the Council of Trent we gather that the dispositions for justification are in a manner the antici-

5. *ST* I-II, q. 113, a. 2.

pation of its effects.[6] Faith, and fear, and hope, and charity, and contrition, which flourish in all their supernatural beauty in the soul that is God's friend, are also the first heralds of the springtime of grace, the first tokens and pledges that the winter of sin is over and gone. Let us, therefore, briefly examine them.

First of all, there is faith. "He that comes to God," says the Apostle, "must believe that He is." We have spoken more than once of the opinions of those who would have us see in this faith nothing but a firm conviction that the holiness of Christ has covered all our sins, and procured for us the certainty of salvation. This is very different from the Catholic teaching. The faith which we assert to be necessary is that faith which will show us how to seek for grace and find it—that faith which alone can lift our minds to the things of God and, showing us His glory and His goodness, awaken in our hearts a longing desire to be the recipients of His blessings by acknowledging Him as the almighty and most gracious Author of grace and the Giver of all good gifts. It is, therefore, really and truly that submission of the mind and heart by which we accept the teaching of God because of His divine authority and infallible truth. And hence it is that the inspired writers so frequently insist on faith as necessary to salvation; indeed, so emphatic is their language, that there are not wanting those who err in consequence and try to believe that faith is the only condition of this great work. A foolish error, truly, for, as we have just been saying, the faith that justifies is a firm belief in the supernatural work of grace, and hence it necessarily leads us on, begetting in us those other dispositions which will complete its work. Hardly has

6. Council of Trent, Session VI, ch. 6.

its saving light broke in upon the sinner's darkened soul, than it shows him those two attributes of God's dread majesty, His justice and His mercy. It shows him sin in all its foulness and the necessary punishment of unrepented sin, and so it generates that holy fear which is the beginning of wisdom. Weak, and at first in many ways imperfect, it gradually mounts higher and becomes more perfect as its motives become more pure, and so it surely accomplishes its necessary work and prepares the soul for perfect charity, which casts out all fear. In this it is encouraged and most wonderfully helped by hope, which ever speaks of mercy and God's unfailing pity and bids him remember always how God's word is pledged to receive the sorrowing and repentant sinner. It tells him of His goodness and unwearied patience, and so it leads him on to love this tender and most gracious Father, and, while grieving bitterly and in all sincerity for all the woeful past, to make a firm and steady resolution to avoid such misery for the future.

This, then, is what we mean by disposing ourselves to receive this gift. Yet we must remember that these dispositions are glorious graces in themselves. "No man can come to me," says our Lord, "except the Father draw him" (John 6:44). All we can do is to cast ourselves down in the dust of our own nothingness and, avowing our unworthiness, implore of God the help we need so much. We can but listen for His footsteps and hasten to open to Him, lest by delaying we should miss Him and He should have passed by. We have to live, to die, and to be judged; and we wish so to live, so to die, so to be judged, that we may receive the crown of everlasting glory—and for all this, we who are born in sin, we who ourselves have sinned so often and so deeply, most surely stand in need of justifying grace. It is at once the pledge and the means of our final success. For those whom God has chosen and predestined to be made like to His only Son, them He also calls; and whom He so calls, He justifies.

VII

Grace and Merit

The state of graces implies the abiding presence of God in the soul. It implies a most special abiding presence, over and above that ordinary indwelling which is common to all God's creatures. In his treatise on the Blessed Trinity, St. Thomas has an article which puts this truth very clearly before us. "God," he says, "is present everywhere by His essence, His presence, and His power. But over and above this ordinary mode of the divine Presence, there is a special way which is peculiar to intellectual beings, for in them God can be present, as the object known is present to the mind, or as the thing loved is linked to the will. And then God is not merely said to be in that creature, but He dwells in it as in His own consecrated temple."[1] These words of the Angelic Doctor seem to sum up the whole doctrine of grace, and to reveal at the same time the secret of its marvelous power. It is God Himself dwelling in the soul and clothing it with His dazzling glory: it is God Himself taking possession of the soul and vivifying it with His almighty power. We remind ourselves of St. Paul, the preacher of grace, and its brightest trophy, and we remember what he was before that journey to Damascus, as we hear him saying, "By the grace of God, I am what I am" (1 Cor. 15:10). We see him bowed down and broken by sufferings and persecutions and trials of every sort, and we listen to his brave profession of faith: "I can do all things in Him who strengthens me" (Phil. 4:13); and, thinking of all this, we begin to understand those other words of his, so truly startling in the apparent bold excess of their confidence and trust: "I know in whom I have believed, and I am certain that there is laid up for me a crown of justice, which my Master will one day bestow upon me, because He is a just Judge" (2 Tim. 1:12; 4:8). In other words, not only does grace change and transform and justify our souls, but it is likewise a principle of merit; it gives such a value to the good works which it inspires that by them we deserve everlasting life; it raises us so high, and makes us so pleasing in the sight of our Creator, that He admits us to a share in His eternal glory, not as a mere favor, but in strict justice, as the merited reward of our labors. But here, at the very outset, we must remind ourselves once more that God is under no obligation to His creatures. He has a right to our service because He is our Creator. But in His loving goodness and mercy He stoops down to us, making our service worthy of His acceptance, worthy of His infinite reward, by gratuitously bestowing upon us the gift of grace, and all those gracious helps which enable us to carry out His merciful designs. The reward is therefore justly merited, and yet it is a grace.

In the last chapter we tried to realize the effect of justifying grace. We saw how it made the soul just before God and holy in His sight. But it is an old saying in the schools that

1. *ST* I, q. 43, a. 3.

operatio sequitur esse, or, in other words, the acts of any agent must be in accordance with its nature; and so, when grace has made the soul just and holy, all its works must be just and holy likewise, and, therefore, meritorious before God. It is this secondary effect of grace that we have now to endeavor to explain.

Merit, strictly speaking, is the consequence of a moral act, implying that it is deserving of praise or blame, reward or punishment; but in ordinary parlance the word is used only in a good sense, and when we speak of a bad act and its consequences we call it demerit. But in whichever sense we use it, or whichever word we employ, we see that it necessarily includes the idea of another person, for whom, or against whom, the act is performed. If there is a real just proportion between the act and its reward, so that the latter can be claimed in justice, then the old scholastics speak of it as *de condigno*, whereas, if such a right does not exist, and the only hope of recompense lies in the kindness of the one obliged, then is it called *de congruo*[2]; and this distinction is in many ways most necessary and most helpful, as we shall see.

But before going any further, it is necessary to remind ourselves of those qualifications which are essential to every act in order that we may suppose it capable of possessing merit in the sight of God. It must of course be voluntary, and it must be good, and accomplished, moreover, for the sake of Him who will reward it. Our common sense rejects, as altogether foolish, the idea of giving full wages to convicts for enforced labor or rewarding a pickpocket for his trouble; and though the scribes and Pharisees were neither convicts nor pickpockets when they so liberally bestowed their alms

2. *ST* I-II, q. 114, a. 6.

at the corners of the streets, yet the act was done for self and not for God. They literally blew their own trumpet; and in that gratification, as our Lord so justly pointed out, they received their only reward. Another very important condition of merit is the state of grace. The soul in mortal sin is God's open and avowed enemy, altogether incapable therefore of deserving His rewards, or of retaining any right to those it may already hold. "If the just man turn from his righteousness, and does iniquity, then all his righteousness shall not be remembered" (Ez. 18:24). Nevertheless, the same inspired Scripture exhorts sinners to do good works by way of moving God to bestow upon them the grace of repentance. "Learn to do well, then come and accuse me, says the Lord. If your sins be as scarlet, they shall be made as white as snow" (Is. 1:17). Moreover, it is in this life only that merit is possible, and so our Blessed Lord urges us to employ well the time at our disposal. "Work while you have the day, for the night comes when no man can work" (John 9:4). And lastly, all merit supposes a promise of recompense on the part of God. "There can be no such thing in man as merit with regard to God," says St. Thomas, "except on the supposition of the divine promise and prearrangement."[3] The laborer in the vineyard may bear the heat and burden of the day, and his labor may seem to deserve its reward; but he has no claim on the master of the vineyard unless he was engaged and employed by him, and the due recompense agreed on.

So much, then, for the nature of merit and its conditions; let us now try to see the bearing of all this on our good works. Surely no one will deny that good works qualified by all these conditions are really meritorious in the sight of God.

---

3. *ST* I-II, q. 114, a. 1.

Even those who reject the Catholic doctrine of grace, and make justification consist in the mere external "apprehension" of the justice and merits of Christ—a theory so cleverly described and refuted in Newman's "Loss and Gain"—even they would admit the possibility of merit in the angels and in unfallen humanity. Further than this, their opinions will not allow them to go, and so they would maintain that, even after justification, man's works are not only incapable of merit, but are in themselves positively offensive in God's sight, though overlooked by Him because of Christ's merits. Hence we must briefly state the Catholic doctrine, which teaches that when once the soul is justified by grace, its supernatural works are meritorious in God's sight, even to the extent of deserving everlasting happiness. The same Almighty God who declared to Abraham that He Himself would be his reward, has also graciously comforted us under our burdens, and bade us be glad and rejoice because our reward is very great in heaven. It was this same reward which St. Paul placed before his persecuted flock. "Our suffering," he said, "which is but momentary, works for us above measure exceedingly, an eternal weight of glory" (2 Cor. 4:17). And He who is Himself that eternal reward appeals directly to us in the Apocalypse. "Behold I come quickly and my reward is with me, to give unto every man according to his works" (Rev. 22:12).

The supernatural works, therefore, which are accomplished by a soul rejoicing in the fullness of the life of grace, really and truly deserve the glory of heaven. They deserve it *de condigno*, that is to say, as we have already explained, as their just reward, if we consider them as the outcome of that supernatural life, and the beautiful fruits of the indwelling of the Holy Spirit; but if, on the contrary, we look at them rather as they are in themselves, as nothing more than the good and reasonable acts of man's free will, then the reward is *de congruo*—the outcome of God's liberality and loving kindness. "It is fitting," says St. Thomas, "and becoming, that God should reward, in the fullness of His magnificence, the works that man has accomplished in the strength of his weakness."[4] But when that same weakness of our poor human nature is supplemented by the supernatural power of grace, when the creature is made partaker of the divine nature and the adopted child of God, then the glory of heaven becomes our rightful inheritance and reward. "You are not now a servant," says St. Paul, "but a son; and if a son, an heir through Christ" (Gal. 4:7). "The spirit himself," he says in another place, "bears witness with our spirit, that we are the children of God; and if children, heirs, heirs of God and joint heirs with Christ" (Rom. 8:16–17). And we must not omit to notice how the Apostle, while extolling the power of grace, repeatedly reminds us of our dependence on Christ. For it is Jesus Christ our Savior who merits heaven for us. He is the source of all our grace, and we only merit it through Him. Our sonship comes through Him and through His infinite merits. And as the purchase-money of this glorious gift was nothing less than His most precious Blood, we at once see its infinite value, its truly infinite power, and how, in consequence, it can communicate to our good works a value that is infinite and make them really worthy of the kingdom of heaven. Notice the words we have used. It makes them *really worthy*. When we say it is our Blessed Lord who merits heaven for us, that it is He who merits in us and by us, we are not following in the footsteps of those of whom we were just

4. *ST* I-II, q. 114, a. 3.

now speaking, nor proclaiming ourselves to be useless or, at the best, but mere machines. "I live," says the Apostle, "now not I, but Christ lives in me" (Gal. 2:20). That is to say, our Lord merits in us and by us, inasmuch as it is He who gives to us the grace to merit, and also moves us to employ it well; and likewise (and most especially) because He is our head, and we His members, and we are united to our Blessed Lord in life and action as the members are united to the head: hence the merit of our actions, so entirely due to Him, is at the same time most really and truly our own. Thus, as the days and weeks and years pass by, and we struggle onwards, falling, it may be, time after time, and yet ever rising again to look towards the eternal mountains whence help will come in our hour of need, if we but ask for it, we can, and we may most surely hope for final victory because of our poor persevering struggle and our patient efforts. Our hopes do not rest on those efforts, and in the merits they acquire, yet we hope because of them, seeing in them the withered stalks and shrivelled leaves from which the grace of God will one day weave our glorious crown, when the touch of His hand shall have given to them a beauty all divine.

Now, following up the rule which has hitherto always guided us in these brief chapters, we must analyze the subject still more closely, and endeavor to discover the first principle on which all supernatural merit stands. In the fifth chapter we defined a principle as that from which anything else proceeded, and when we speak of the principle of a meritorious act, or indeed of any act whatever, we see at once that it is necessary to make a distinction between a remote principle which only gives the power of acting, and a proximate principle which really elicits the act. A dead man can never see, no matter how perfect may be the organs of sight in his body;

and, on the other hand, if the eyes have been destroyed, sight is altogether impossible to the living man, no matter how perfect may be the workings of his mind. It needs no arguments to convince us that nature left to itself can never be the principle of merit, however remote we may consider it. "Even as the branch," says our Lord, "can never bring forth fruit of itself, if cut off from the vine, so neither can you, unless you remain in me. Without me you can do nothing" (John 15:4) And indeed, taking nature at its very best, as St. Thomas so justly points out, it could never deserve eternal life, because no cause or principle can produce an effect which exceeds its own nature and is utterly beyond its powers.[5] But eternal life is in every way supernatural, above nature, as St. Paul reminds us in those beautiful words: "Eye has not seen, nor ear heard, neither has it entered into the heart of man to conceive, what things God has prepared for them that love Him" (1 Cor. 2:9). But if we take into account the work of sin, the impossibility becomes more evident. Not only can our nature never merit eternal life, but it has deserved eternal death. "The wages of sin is death" (Rom. 6:23). Left to ourselves, our works are absolutely valueless, as St. Paul reminds us, no matter how grand they may seem in themselves. We may preach the Word of God and convert thousands, we may throw away our riches in acts of charity, we may pass our lives in the most humbling mortifications, and even sacrifice them at the call of duty; but if grace be absent from our souls, *nihil mihi prodest*—it is all of no use—"it profits me nothing" (1 Cor. 13:2). But with grace all is changed. Great things are no longer necessary, or rather, the smallest things become great, and by a kind look, a friendly word, a sympathetic act, a cup

5. *ST* I-II, q. 114, a. 2.

of cold water given to a poor beggar man—we can merit everlasting happiness. Grace, then, is most certainly the remote principle of all merit; and charity, or the love of God, is the proximate principle, for when we were speaking of the primary conditions of merit, we laid down three at least which love alone can fulfill in all their perfection. We said that the act must be the free offering of the will, for otherwise God will not accept it. "This people honors me with their lips, but their heart is far from me," and the first and best offering the will can make is the offering of love. We said that the act must be good. No work can be completely good without love, since love seeks ever the last end on which all goodness depends. We said that there must be also that mutual arrangement between God and His creatures, for man must act for God and God must accept His service with a view to the reward, and it is by love that God directs man and all His works towards eternal life, which is the end and term of love; and by love also, man devotes himself, and all he has, to the service of God, his last end. Hence love it is which changes and transmutes the baser metals of our acts and turns them into purest gold; and this love is manifested in our lives, not by anything extraordinary or out of the common, but by that general, peaceful, habitual intention of the mind by which we choose God for our last end and try to love Him and serve Him by keeping His commandments. But the more real and actual this love is found to be, the more abundant will be our merit.

Even in this life, recompense varies according to the dignity of the person to be rewarded, and an architect is not paid on the same scale as a bricklayer. The greater our grace, therefore, and consequently the greater our dignity in God's sight, the more abundant will be our reward. It may happen that a hundred people hear the same Mass, and one receives a hundredfold more than all the rest put together, because he has accumulated more grace and is in consequence more pleasing in God's sight. And even supposing all heard the Mass with exactly the same attention and devotion, the one who was highest in grace would receive a higher reward, for when we offer to God our works, we offer ourselves also, and hence the more abundant our grace, the richer and the more acceptable is the offering we make to God. How foolish, then, to undervalue or neglect in any way this precious grace, when it can do so much for us! How reckless and how criminal to content ourselves with leading lives that we consider decent and respectable, when with so little effort we can increase, to an unspeakable degree, God's glory and our own everlasting reward! Just think: A little thing that we can hardly notice at the time, is capable of changing our eternity! For instance, something done for God once a day, say, our attendance at Mass, to which we are not obliged or to which we only come to please our loving and most generous Master: Who can measure the reward that He will give for that? Supposing it to be the very least that He would give—one solitary degree of grace—a month of such attendance would mean thirty such degrees, a year three hundred and sixty-five, and every single degree means an increase in our everlasting reward, so great that our mind cannot imagine it. And when, instead of one solitary act like hearing Mass, we contemplate a life that is passed in the sunlight of God's grace, and try to calculate its daily acts—prayers, Mass, visits to the Blessed Sacrament, the hours of study, the journeys to and fro, the pleasant recreations, and then realize that every moment of such a day, and every single act, no matter how ordinary, has its accompanying grace—we get some idea of the exceedingly great reward awaiting such a soul, and some idea also of the awful loss that is the fate of one who chooses, as he thinks, to please himself, and lead an "ordinary" life, and take things easily. Lucky may he think himself if he escape eternal loss and everlasting ruin, for God will not allow us to bury our talent in the earth. When we stand before Him to give an account of our lives, it will be of no avail to plead that we have done no harm: we must do good. No harm! Idleness is harm, carelessness is harm, indifference is harm, the worst harm of all, the harm that will draw down upon us that scathing condemnation: "You wicked and slothful servant, out of your own mouth do I condemn you" (Luke 19:20). Not to value our privileges, not to be jealous of them, not to be eager to share them with others, all this is a downright insult to Him who has bestowed them upon us, who has snatched us like brands from the burning. And the just punishment of such contempt is to be abandoned by God, and given up to a reprobate sense. "To everyone that has shall be given, but from him that has not, even that which he seems to have shall be taken away" (Luke 19:26).

How clearly does all this show our utter dependence on God! How vividly it puts before us the necessity of distrusting ourselves, for if this glorious treasure of grace is ours, we carry it about through the midst of many dangers—in earthen vessels, to teach us that its excellence is of God and not of ourselves. It is quite true that grace merits more grace, in ever-increasing abundance, and by perseverance in grace we can justly deserve the glory of heaven; but—and here is the thought that sobers us and makes as tremble—the first grace that came to us in this world to set our faces heavenward was God's free gift, and the last grace that touches us, as we close our eyes in death, and that leads us through the dark valley is equally gratuitous! Who, then, can dare to presume? And if we listen to the tempter's voice, and foolishly despise the riches of God's mercy, for the empty, passing pleasures of a life of sin, we sign the warrant of our own rejection. For once in the state of sin, as we have said, the merits and the graces of the past are ours no longer, and salvation becomes impossible unless God work a miracle of mercy and call us back to Him—and this we cannot merit, or even beg for, unless He move us to it. What folly, then, to run a risk so awful! And if, on the other hand, our lives are free from all this misery, and we are walking in the way of God's commandments, we need His help to *persevere*! It is not enough to serve Him in our boyhood only—we must cling to Him in youth, in manhood and old age, even to the very end, "He only that perseveres to the end shall be saved," and this again is God's free grace. "It is God," says St. Paul, "who works in you both to will and to accomplish according to His good will." "With fear and trembling, therefore," says the same apostle, "work out your salvation." Surely, then, we must distrust ourselves and lean on God. To persevere is but to use the means so freely given to us. It is to live under the shadow of God's wings, it is to be safe in the company of our divine Master, and there is no condemnation for them that are in Christ Jesus. The crown of life is waiting for us, if only we are faithful unto death. It is ours already because of our grace, and can only be lost by losing grace. "Hold fast, therefore, that which you have, that no man take your crown" (Rev. 3:11).

VIII

Gratia Dei Vita Aeterna

When a certain anxious soul, often wavering between fear and hope, did once, being oppressed with grief, most humbly cast himself down in prayer before one of the altars in the church, and pondering over these things, did say within himself, 'Oh, if I only knew that I should persevere,' he straightaway heard within himself the voice of God rejoicing. And if you did know, what would you do? Do now what you would then do, and you shall be perfectly secure."[1] These words of the devout author of the *Imitation* put before us the greatest mystery of grace, the last question we have to examine, the last problem we must try to solve—a mystery, a question, a problem, briefly summed up by the Apostle in those familiar words, "gratia Dei vita aeterna"—the grace of God, or the fruit of the grace of God, is everlasting life. In the first chapter we declared that our purpose and intention was to contemplate, as closely as we could, the wonderful mystery of God's dealings with His creatures. We admitted the difficulty of the task, we even granted at the very outset that complete success was quite impossible! Step by step we have advanced under the safe guidance of our faith and reason, and now we stand upon the very summit, where our reason, blinded by the glory of Him who dwells in unapproachable light, falls prostrate in trembling adoration, our faith alone remaining to hold us up and strengthen us to stand erect and gaze upon the brightness, and cry aloud in spite of human weakness, *Credo*—I believe!

We know that God created us for no other end than to know Him, to love Him, to serve Him in this world, in order that we may live eternally with Him in the world to come. We have seen how, in pursuance of this grand design, He has raised us to a supernatural state, and crowned us with the gift of grace. We have seen how much we need this glorious gift of our Creator, and how it acts upon our fallen being. We tried to understand its marvelous nature, its causes, and its beautiful effects; and, having studied it so closely, we would now withdraw, and standing, as it were, afar off, endeavor to behold it in its Uncreated Source and Fountain Head—the Eternal God Himself. For manifestly there are two ways of looking at God's works. We may consider them in themselves, as they exist in time, in all their varied order and succession, their changes and their actions and sufferings, as they gradually progress, thus attaining the purpose of their being, or failing in its accomplishment; or we may go back to the mind of Him who made them, and we shall see how there, in that eternal present, the order is reversed, and what seemed first is last, and the effect is seen to be the cause. In the former case we have before us God's dominion working out its purposes, His divine government in action; in the latter those same mysterious purposes are gathered up in one

1. Thomas à Kempis, *Imitation of Christ*, Book I, 25.

eternal act, arranging and disposing all things for an end, and this we call God's providence. But in the case of man, the end proposed is supernatural, or quite beyond the reach of all created powers. Hence, as we have seen, God gives us supernatural means, proportioned to this end; His infinite knowledge shows Him who, amongst His creatures, will avail themselves of those same means, and so obtain the crown of life, and who amongst them will voluntarily turn aside; and this foreknowledge of success and preparation of reward is called "predestination." It is a word of many meanings, a word expressing many thoughts, which fascinate as much as they repel. It is the definition of a mystery, but a mystery of which our reason shows us much, and faith still more, like all the other mysteries revealed by God to man. Moreover, in the elucidation of this mystery, we are free to follow different teachers, offering different explanations, for though the Church insists upon the dogma, she has not explained it, but allows the various schools of saints and holy men and learned doctors to use their best endeavors for that end. And if you ask, as some have done, why this is so, and what can be the use of argument in such a matter, we must answer first of all, that knowledge for its own sake is a good to be desired and striven for, and anything that treats of God is knowledge in its highest sense; and in the next place we may put it forward as the best reply to that most foolish calumny which accuses us of stifling reason. We bow before the mysteries of faith, and salute them with a loyal, frank submission, and then we turn upon them the searchlight of our reason and use on them the intellectual powers that God has given us. Schools and systems are not the Church. Their voices must be hushed in silence when she begins to speak, for she proclaims the truths of faith, which they but try to understand; and it would be the height of folly to refuse the dogma because we do not care for this or that, or any explanation of it.

To return, then, to predestination. We take it here to mean the divine pre-ordination by which Almighty God prepares eternal glory for certain souls, to whom He therefore gives the means by which they may obtain it. It is also called in Holy Scripture God's "election," or God's "purpose," and there is hardly to be found a single book of Sacred Scripture in which this mystery of faith is not most clearly put before us. "My sheep hear my voice," said our Lord, "and they shall not perish everlastingly, and no one shall snatch them out of my hand" (John 10:27). "Come, ye blessed of my Father," He says in another place, "receive the Kingdom prepared for you from before the foundation of the world." So also St. Paul, in his epistle to the Ephesians, calls upon them to "bless God, the Father of our Lord Jesus Christ, who has predestined us unto the adoption of children, according to the purpose of His will" (Eph. 1:5, 11); and again, "In Christ we are called by lot, being predestined according to the purpose of Him, who works all things according to His will." Hence the reasoning of St. Thomas is brief, but to the point. God, who cannot change in any way, has determined from all eternity all that He does in time. One of His acts in time is to create, sanctify, and bring to everlasting life the soul of man. Therefore from all eternity He decreed to do that, and this eternal prearrangement is predestination.

But before going any further, I may as well anticipate a difficulty almost too foolish to deserve consideration, but which faces us continually, no matter what system or explanation we may adopt. The whole theory of predestination, you may say, is fatal to our liberty, and destructive of all work, all activity, and all morality. If God from all eternity has settled those who are to be amongst the saved, and those who are to be amongst the lost, why should we take any trouble? Why attempt to *work* out our salvation with fear and trembling? No matter what we do, we cannot change decrees that are *eternal*! Now I have called this a difficulty, although I said that it was foolish, and hardly worthy of the name, so easy is the answer. Predestination is a part of providence, and, therefore, while it specifies a certain end, it necessarily includes the means. The crown of glory which God has destined for His chosen ones is meant to be a hardly earned reward, given only to those who persevere to the end. No one can be crowned, but those who have striven manfully; no one can claim to reach those gates of life, but those who tread the straight and narrow way. What should we think of one who hoped to pass an all-important examination, and yet refused to study hard because his final failure or success was already known to God?

What sort of farmer would he be who would let the ploughshare rust, and leave fields untilled, because the next year's crops and harvests are already portioned out by Him who is the Lord of all, to whom belongs the earth and all its fullness? When, therefore, God from all eternity decreed what was to be, He also linked together causes and effects, nor is the effect decreed in any other way than through and with the cause—be it free, necessary, or contingent. The real difficulty, after all, lies in the motive. Why does God in this most special way choose certain souls, and do so much for them, while others are allowed to choose eternal ruin? Here is the difficulty, the *nodus intricatissimus totius theologiae*, the Gordian knot of all theology; and if we cannot hope to cut it or untie it, we can at least examine it, and see what can be said about it.

Time will not allow us to discuss the rambling and impossible suggestions of those outside the Church, the Manichaeans and Pelagians of every sort and shade, who either deny free will altogether or venture to exalt it at the expense of God's omnipotence. We can accept no explanation which in any way may seem to trespass on these two most certain truths, and so we will begin with that which here, as elsewhere, claims the place of honor, and deserves it if only for the sake of him whose name it bears—the explanation of St. Thomas and his followers. You may perhaps remember how, in the first chapter, when we treated of free will in contact with divine Omnipotence, we showed how Thomists tried to solve the difficulty by appealing to the efficacious will of God, and making its efficiency the cause of liberty. And in the fourth chapter, when there was question of explaining how it was that grace could move the will of man without in any way entrenching on its freedom, it was to this same will of God that we were told to look. So now, when searching for the motive of this choice, which we have called predestination, the answer of the Thomist school, to be consistent, must be still the same—the Almighty Will of God. Here, then, is the explanation. God knows all things because He sees all things. He sees them in Himself, because He is the first and universal cause. We could not say that God was forced to get His knowledge from outside Himself: the very thought would be a sacrilege. With this principle as our starting point, we may go on to argue that if God sees all things, He must see the future acts of our free will; and He sees these also, as we showed in the first chapter, because He is their first great cause, and could not see them otherwise. God cannot see in my free will, what I am going to do tomorrow, because it is not there. Free will is indeterminate and indifferent until it acts. Nor can He see my future doings in the various motives, causes, or surrounding circumstances which may act upon my will; a knowledge based on that alone could only be conjectural. Yet it is certain that He does know all that I shall do tomorrow, and the only logical conclusion is to admit that He sees them because He wills them. "I am God," He says, "who show from the beginning the things that shall be at last, and from ancient times the things that are not yet done, saying, my counsel shall stand, and all my will shall be done" (Is. 46:10). And remember how we answered those who try to make believe that this is fatalism. "Infallibly" and "necessarily" are words with very different meanings!

Applying all this, then, to the mystery of predestination, we lay down as a general principle that God desires the salvation of all His reasonable creatures, and in His goodness gives to all the necessary means. Many fail, for the natural weakness of our being is increased by sin and all its woeful consequences, and if the proffered help of grace be spurned, eternal ruin is inevitable. But by a special act of mercy and most gracious pity, God vouchsafes to choose out certain ones, and secure them for Himself. They are His "*elect.*" Underneath them are the everlasting arms, and, as a consequence of this most loving care, they persevere and win the crown prepared for them from all eternity. For the choice which saved them was eternal and gratuitous! It was not because in life they tried so hard to keep God's law, and really kept it; not in consequence of their merits, therefore, that they were thus singled out; but, being chosen out of God's pure mercy, He willed that they should do all this, and so secure the crown. From all eternity God knew His beloved ones; He knew them because He had chosen them, and prepared this glory for them. So, in His own good time, their life on earth began, and His mercy went before them, and guarded them in all their ways; and so surely, yet with the most absolute freedom, they slowly worked out their salvation with fear and trembling. All things worked for this one great end. "All things work together unto good," says St. Paul, "for such as are called according to His purpose" (Rom. 8:30); and in all their lives there was not an act, however insignificant and lowly it might be, that had not been already counted up and weighed in the balance, and made to have its special share and do its special work in meriting that great reward. All these things, therefore—all our works and sufferings and merits and graces—are not the causes, but the effects, of that glorious choice of God. "Those whom God foreknew," says St. Paul—*πρωεγνω*, that is, those whom God has chosen as His vessels of election, for the word St. Paul uses has this special meaning—"them He also predestined to be made conformed to the image of His Son;" and then, noting the various steps by which this choice is manifested and carried out, the great apostle continues, "and those whom He predestined, them He also called; and whom He called, them He justified; and whom He justified, them He also glorified"(Rom. 8:28).

Thus, according to the Thomist school, the motive of predestination is God's glory. Predestination is the crowning work of grace, the perfect work of grace, and grace alone. For grace, in the opinion of St. Thomas, and as we have tried to show in all these chapters, is not simply a supernatural touch, depending for its full effect on our free will, or on our surrounding circumstances; it is not a mere whispering of that still, small voice from which we can and do so often turn away; not a passing glow of fervor which enables us to triumph over present difficulties—but it is that supernatural, direct, immediate impulse from Almighty God, executing in time those manifold decrees that from the beginning of the days of eternity have infallibly decided all future acts. It is God Himself directly working in and on our will, and *effecting* our co-operation, that the merit may be all our own; "God Himself," says St. Thomas, "*who acts immediately in every agent without excluding the action of nature or free will.*"[2] Hence predestination includes both the last end and the means necessary to obtain that end, that is to say, our merits; and, as commonsense would tell us, the end is not for the sake of the means, but the means are given and are used for the sake of the end. "What have you," asks St. Paul, "that you have not received?" And then, in equally clear and emphatic language, he goes on to remind us that it is not our efforts, not our strength, not our will, that entitles us to claim the everlasting crown, but God's pure mercy: *Non est volentis, neque currentis; sed miserentis Dei.*[3] And it is God's most perfect work! Why criticize failures where the success is so glorious? Would you blame the University because so many fail, and not rather praise it because of those who win its highest honors? There are souls in hell; yes, but God did not send them there, much less predestine them to such a fate. "He deals patiently, not willing that any should perish, but that all should return to penance" (2 Pet. 3:9); and in another place God Himself assures us that if we fail we have only ourselves to blame: *Perditio tua ex te.* Still, you say, He could have saved them—why did He not do it? He could have worked a miracle for them, and even at the last hour

2. Thomas Aquinas, *De potentia*, q. 3, a. 7.
3. "Not of him that wills, nor of him that runs, but of God that shows mercy."

drawn them to Himself—why did He not do it? He could save all the world—why does He not do it? "O man!" says St. Paul, "who are you that replies against God?" (Rom. 9:20). And then, as though the very greatness of the mystery had cast him in the dust before his Maker, he cries out: "O the depth of the riches of the wisdom and of the knowledge of God! How incomprehensible are His judgments, and how unsearchable His ways! For who has known the mind of the Lord, and who has been His counsellor? For of Him, and by Him, and in Him, are all things; to Him be glory forever" (Rom. 11:33–36).

To turn now to another view, which places the motive of predestination in the merits of our free will. It first saw light about the sixteenth century, when Calvin dared to claim for his outrageous theories the authority of St. Thomas. It is the explanation offered by a school which has been, and is still, the home of saints and apostolic men and most devoted sons of Holy Church. To them it seemed that Thomism made difficulties by its love of logic and consistency, and in its fervent zeal for God's glory somewhat underrated man's free will. If mystery there must be, they urged, why not leave it on the side of God, of whom we know so little, rather than on the side of our own liberty—the very essence of our life! Surely, they urge, it is not enough to prove that we are masters of our free acts; we want to *feel* it, and so, they go on to say, without troubling as to the why, or how, or wherefore, let us suppose that somehow or other God knows all the future, and all that we should do in any sort of circumstances, or with any sort of graces. Let us take this for granted, and then say that, having given to all sufficient grace, He looks to see how each will use it, and, seeing some who do their best to profit by it, He predestines them to glory. The grace He gives, moreover, is not, as the Thomists say, immediate motion from Almighty God, but an indifferent help, sufficient to enable us to keep God's law, provided our free will decide to use it. Of course, the first grace is gratuitous—that must be granted; and the gift of final perseverance is gratuitous likewise, and it is not very easy to explain why God refuses to place all in equal circumstances, so that all their equal graces may have equal chances; but taking it all in all, it seems an easier theory than the Thomist one, and certainly is more indulgent to free will.

It may appear an easier theory, and it doubtless is more flattering to free will; but are these advantages so great, and so essential, as to justify us in adopting as our own a theory and an explanation which seems, at all events, to compromise God's infinite knowledge and supreme dominion? But be this as it may, whatever system we elect to follow, and whatever motive we may venture to imagine, we must believe that God predestines His elect. He chooses them, and everlasting happiness is the consequence of His choice. Put away, then, for a moment, schools and systems, and see what we believe! First of all, we hold most firmly that when God spoke His word of power, and man became a living soul, it was to bless and not to curse our race that He gave it being. "He wills all men to be saved, and to come unto the knowledge of the truth" (1 Tim. 2), and therefore was it that He took upon Himself our human nature and died for all. And not only does He wish to save us, but He gives us all-sufficient help. He does not leave us to ourselves, but wisely governs us and all our acts. Moreover, we believe that since the end for which He made us is supernatural, the means are supernatural likewise, and therefore the successful attainment of this end is a most special act of Providence which we call Predestination. We believe that though this help is supernatural, and hence in every way gratuitous, it is a real principle of merit which God rewards, and a reason for grave punishment if contemptuously despised. We believe this help is given to all, though all will not accept it; and, therefore, such as obstinately persist in their rebellion, merit reprobation, which is not their pre-ordained fate, but the consequence of their sin. There is nothing hard in this. Our difficulties are mainly due to our imperfect knowledge of God. We judge of Him as we should judge of our poor selves. We use our ideas and our lights, we measure Him by our duties, laws, and obligations, whereas He is the one necessary Being, first, free, independent in every way, the absolute law of all! We are complex, God is simple. We live in time, God in eternity. We remember the past, and imagine the future; with God there is neither past nor future—He sees past and future now! So God sees what He will do, or rather what He is doing, a hundred years hence, and yet He is absolutely free! And if we know so little about God, what do we know about ourselves? We are individuals amongst unnumbered millions. To explain fully, or completely, we ought to examine all. If then, after all, we know so little about these two extremes—the Creator and the creature, God and man—is it astonishing that we fail to explain their exact relationship, their point of contact? The only thing is to believe; and belief is not ignorance, but perfect knowledge. Only a fool rejects what he cannot understand. Faith and reason tell us of a God, infinitely perfect, Creator and Ruler of all; they tell us also of creatures endowed with reason and free will, and consequent responsibility for good and evil. These two truths cannot oppose each other: they must combine somehow. It may not be easy to see how, but we know they must, because they are true. It is the height of folly to deny what is clear because we fail to understand something which is hidden.

Our business, therefore, is to bow down humbly before the impenetrable veil of the divine mysteries, knowing that in His own good time God will draw it aside, and make all things clear. Meantime, we have not to trouble ourselves about God's designs, but rather look to our execution of them, laboring, as St. Peter says, "that by good works we may make our calling and election sure" (1 Pet. 1:20). For predestination is but another name for final perseverance, and to persevere means the diligent employment of the necessary means. Look, then, into your own lives. Some of you try hard to keep God's law; you live beneath the shadow of His wings; His word is a lamp unto your feet, and a light on your pathway. You are proud to call yourselves His faithful servants. *Gaudete ex exultate*! It is a sign that should rejoice your hearts—a token of the everlasting joy that awaits you. And there are others around us who hardly ever give a thought to God, who please themselves in all they do, and utterly despise the pleadings of divine Grace. It is their own free choice, and it is a choice that makes us fear and tremble, for it is a sign of reprobation and eternal ruin. It is for us to do our best, and leave the issue in God's hands. "Be faithful unto death, and I will give you the crown of life" (Rev. 2:10).

CLUNY MEDIA

Designed by Fiona Cecile Clarke, the Cluny Media *logo depicts a monk at work in the scriptorium, with a cat sitting at his feet.*

The monk represents our mission to emulate the invaluable contributions of the monks of Cluny in preserving the libraries of the West, our strivings to know and love the truth.

The cat at the monk's feet is Pangur Bán, from the eponymous Irish poem of the 9th century. The anonymous poet compares his scholarly pursuit of truth with the cat's happy hunting of mice. The depiction of Pangur Bán is an homage to the work of the monks of Irish monasteries and a sign of the joy we at Cluny take in our trade.

"Messe ocus Pangur Bán,
cechtar nathar fria saindan:
bíth a menmasam fri seilgg,
mu memna céin im saincheirdd."

Made in the USA
Middletown, DE
05 September 2021

46883240R00149